Dr. York
The Truth
BIOGRAPHICAL REBUTTAL TO *PEOPLE MAGAZINE*

Revelation Chapter 12:7-9

"And there was war in heaven: **Michael and His Angels** *fought against the dragon; and the dragon fought and his angels, And prevailed not; neither was their place found any more in heaven. And the great dragon was cast out, that old serpent, called the Devil, and Satan, which deceiveth the whole world; he was cast out into the earth, and his angels were cast out with him."*

DonVito Harold Long

DR. YORK -THE TRUTH.

Copyright © 2020 by DonVito H. Long.

All rights reserved. Printed in the United States of America. No part of this book may be used or reproduced in any manner whatsoever without prior permission in writing from the author or publisher except in the case of brief quotation in critical articles or reviews. For more information write to:

Crystal City Publishing Company
P.O. BOX 36761
Grosse Pointe Farms, Mi 48236

    Or email

CrystalCityPublishingCompany@gmail.com

ALL RIGHTS RESERVED

NOTICE
All images and excerpts used and contained in and on this book are for critic, teaching and research purposes under the doctrine of "fair use."

ISBN Hardback 978-1-7363933-0-7
ISBN Paperback 978-1-7363933-1-4

Publisher's Cataloging-in-Publication Data

Names: Long DonVito Harold.
Title: Dr. York, the truth: Biographical rebuttal to People magazine / DonVito Harold Long.
Description: Includes bibliographical references. | Grosse Pointe Farms, MI: Crystal City Publishing Company LLC, 2021.
Identifiers: LCCN: 2020925879 | ISBN: 978-1-7363933-0-7 | 978-1-7363933-1-4
Subjects: LCSH York, Malachi, 1945-. | Nubian Islamic Hebrews--History. | Nuwaubian movement--United States--History. | Native Americans--Religion. | BISAC BIOGRAPHY & AUTOBIOGRAPHY / Religious
Classification: LCC BP605.N89 L66 2021 | DDC 299.6/8973/092--dc23

Table of Contents

Foreword v

Introduction xvii

I.D. Channel - People Magazine - Investigates Cults - Factual Rebuttal to the Slander 1

Letter No. 1 from Niki (Nicole Lopez) 57

Letter No. 2 from Niki (Nicole Lopez) 61

Dr. York's Influence 85

Affidavit of Habiybah Washington 119

Habiybah Washington Recant Video 127

Final Argument by Adrian Patrick - The Lead Trial Attorney for Dr. Malachi Z. York 155

Conclusion 175

About the Author 177

Bibliography 179

Foreword

This "man" that you see on the front cover is by no means an ordinary man. He has been referred to as The Man Of Miracles In This Day And Time by many who have borne witness to the powers that come through him. Although he would tell you that his miracle is in his pen (the words of truth he writes); Let me share a few testimonies of the extra-ordinary deeds that has come through this rare occurrence known by many as Dr. York.

Keith Randolph McIntosh

"One day while sitting in class, Al Imaam Isa (Dr. York) started to move his fingers and hand in a rotating motion and then with his right hand he placed his right thumb on the forehead of some of our brothers sitting in the front row, when he removed his thumb a couple of seconds later, a thumb print of a creamish color substance was on my brothers foreheads. Our beloved guide of the world told us it was a Sacred Ash, and that it came from the other side and it held healing properties in it. It amazed me! I have never seen anything like it done at all in my forty-odd years of life. Out of nowhere, Al Maulana (Dr. York) pulled this Sacred Dust. He performed this unique feat (Miracle) with our children in the Masjid, also. As we were coming out of the Masjid, I made it my business to look at the heads of our children and some brothers. There it was, a thumb print of Sacred Ash. As Sayyid Al Imaam Isa Al Haadi Al Mahdi (Dr. York) did perform these things in my presence."

Linda Merritt

"*A handful of us sat attentively listening to the man who sat in front of us. He appeared quite comfortable and well composed in his chair. As his serene yet exuberant voice travelled throughout the room, we waited in anticipation for what he had to say. He began to tell us about himself, an Avatar, and the reason he was here. Fascinated by his words we couldn't help but remember: He said this would be the year we would know who this great man might be. We learned that it was us, who willed him here. He told us he was from another Galaxy, and like him, there are other Avatars that are sent to each part of the world to guide the people. He said that an Avatar does not necessarily have a religion but he teaches LOVE. We must Learn to Love: To Love the trees, birds, and flowers. He explained that an Avatar can transfer your soul to the other side, perform miracles, and make things manifest from the other side. While sitting in front of us, he made movements with his hands and Sacred Ash appeared. He said it comes from Paradise. During the days of old the Sacred Ash was used as a purification, people would put it on their tongue, and it was also put in the location of the third eye. He welcomed us to take some of the Sacred Ash and place it on our Foreheads. Seeing that some of us moved somewhat slowly, he placed some on his forehead to reassure us that it was alright. The entire time while his eyes were glittering and his appearance was that of a very spiritual being radiating positive energy. After Leaving him we all took something with us; our own personal miracle.*"

Earlean Jackson

"*In February 1983, There was a tragedy in which several (3) brothers were stabbed. One brother was stabbed several times, critically injuring him. He was rushed to Wyckoff Hospital along with the others. The Doctor listed him in critical condition. He had a fatal wound below his heart to his liver, with part of it torn away. Bleeding profusely and needing a blood transfusion, he was lying there with oxygen tubes running down his nose, I.V.'s in his arms. Tubes throughout his body and hooked up to an EKG machine. Oh,* how terrible an accident to leave him on his death bed. The very same day, As Sayyid Al Imaam Isa Al Haadi Al Mahdi (Dr. York) comforted him and embraced him with his blessings. He assured him that regardless of what the Doctors diagnosed, He would be alright, and that he would live through all of this. The next day he was fully conscious and talking. The third day he was talking and eating. Within a weeks time, he was out of the Intensive Care Unit. The following week, he was out of the Hospital, back home and feeling fine. He was surely proven to be a miracle, In Medical as well as Religious terms. The Doctors called it a Miraculous Recovery in Medical History. What do you say?"

George Wesley Wallace
"The date was June 26, 1972, The Birthday of our beloved Guide and Teacher. The Masjid complex was located at 452 Rockaway Ave, between Pitkins and Belmont Avenue. We wanted to surprise him with a cake and Gifts, which were located downstairs in the room called "The Upper Room." Brothers locked him in his office so he could be detained long enough for everyone to be ready to surprise him. I remember clearly his saying, "**YOU CAN'T HOLD ME.**" Of course, I didn't pay attention to that because as far as I was concerned he couldn't get out of the office while brothers were guarding the entrance and the sisters were at the stairway sitting on the stairs so he could not walk down. After I walked downstairs to the waiting brothers, sisters and children, to my surprise and amazement, he was walking into the "Upper Room" laughing at us as if to say, "If you want to surprise me by locking me in a room, you're going to have to use a more convincing method."

Jessie Hill
"One night The MOTHERSHIP appeared. Imaam (Dr. York) asked everyone to go outside and look up at it. It was a giant light up in the sky and it covered the whole sky in a circle. Just to look up at it made my heart drop, It was a touching experience. The next day Imaam (Dr. York) told the brothers to tear the minarets

down because the Elders informed him it wasn't properly built. This happened when we first built our Masjid."

Cheryl Franklin
"In the Spring of 1979, We, The community received some damaging accusations from neighbors concerning our "CULTISH" ways. It had made the news and we looked really bad. The next day Imaam (Dr. York) informed us that The Most High had favored us, and that we would be the eventual winners."

Dr. York needs his side of the story to be told. I'm well aware that it will be met with doubt, ridicule and slander. That's okay because all the Messengers of The Almighty went through the same trials and tribulations; Just know and remember this Saying of Dr. York **"Don't say you were not told; Say I was not listening."** The following account is in Dr. York's own words and I quote:

"What I am about to tell you is the Truth. You must let it be known, it is time. I know you will doubt this Story. I know I would if it was not me, myself. I am going to tell you something I never told anyone. My very first encounter with 3 Aliens was October 12th 1955 A.D. I was 10 years old in Teaneck, New Jersey, it was night, I was coming back from Brooklyn, New York seeing family. It was cold, dark, I had to walk from the the bus stop to the house where I lived. As I walked, I saw a bright light above me, a craft. I could not move. A ramp extended from it, it was not very big then I saw what looked like a shadow of a child not bigger than I was, yet then I noticed these big, black bee-like eyes and a big head, long arms and fingers. I wanted to run yet I could not move. Then I noticed 2 others come down the ramp. The first came right up to me and put its fingers right above my eyes at my brow. The fear was gone. It spoke inside my head and said, "We will not hurt you, I am Saaatt, that is what I am called." He turned and pointed at the other two, "That is Alomaaar, she is my sister and he is Krlll." I could see the spelling of their names as he spoke. He said, "We arrived on this planet September 1955 A.D. in Kentucky, we were sent to find you, we will need you."

At 10 years old I did not understand. They each touched me, looked in my eyes and all at once said, "Yes, we found him, this is he." Alomaaar took my hand, led me up the ramp into the craft. I don't know how long I was there. They put something up in my nose, it hurt at first then Saaatt touched my face again. The pain left, they showed me around the craft. There were others of them who looked at me yet, said nothing. One of them I don't remember said, "We will be with you from time to time. Your race sent us, they will also come to you once you're of age to better understand." Then like a flash, I was back on the road alone. I was confused, felt strange yet did not think that had happened. My nose used to bleed a lot. One night in my bedroom, it began to bleed a lot, soon after they came right through the wall of my bedroom, adjusted it and the bleeding stopped. They stayed with me that night, talked with me. I asked them where they were from and they told me. That is when one told me they landed in Kelly, Kentucky September 12, 1955 A.D. and one of them was shot and died so they took her back to the craft. They became my Trusted Friends. They would come often and said, "You can tell people yet they will not accept it." I tried and that was true.

In time they took me. I was around 15 in 1960 A.D., they saw I was doing bad things as a teen, so they took me upon a craft up into a real big craft, I mean really big, there I met my own race "Rizqiyians" who are 9 feet tall, dark-skinned with kind eyes. They taught me yet, I would forget, or I thought I forgot things, I felt it were dreams. By 1963 A.D. I knew I was not like others yet I did not want to be different. I drank wine, hung out with friends, ended up in reforming programs for 3 years. In 1967 A.D. I was home and was told to find Shaikh Dawud, "He will tell you what you are." I found him at 143 State Street. He told me. From then on I knew who I was, my race would come. I was told "Your name is Yaanuwn." I was taken to our planet Rizq in Illiyuwn, I saw so much and they downloaded 76 trillion years of their time in to my mind, I knew things.

One night as I walked home from work in Brooklyn, I stopped by my sister's apartment. When I left on my way from the subway a tall being came up beside me. He told me he was Al Khidr and that he *will soul into mine, that I will become a teacher of many. He spoke Arabic and at the time I did not know Al Khidr and Melchizedek were one and the same. He said, "You will have many visitors over time and when you think to know a thing it will come to you, just speak, we will speak by way of you. Your life will be hard, stay with it no matter what." By the way Earthlings killed Saaatt in Australia and the other two in America in 2015. I am really blessed to be used this way most of my life. I am the Ancient of Days. I have seen worlds born and worlds die, Planets born and planets die. These eyes have seen so very much, this mind knows so very much. I did ask them why they landed in Kentucky, they said it's been being used for thousands of years. The mountains and coverings are so great and the clouds over the forests are good. They said many Star People come and go from there and other places. It is now that time, most people these days accept as fact UFO's as well as ET's. Back then they did not, now even all the old timers of our old school teachings now see all they were taught come to past."*

~ The Master Teacher Dr. Malachi Z. York

Being there is a concentrated effort on behalf of adverse forces to stop Dr. York who is here to raise your level of consciousness so that when the Mothership or Crystal City returns, you will be ready; I will quote Dr. York to convey in part what he has been teaching since 1970 A.D. to prepare you for these days and times.

"Extraterrestrial beings exist in our Universe and on Earth. Some of these beings are here to take over and some are here to help you, so you may not destroy yourselves...Star Wars movies were created to make everyone disbelieve the fact that Extraterrestrials do exist and they do come to this planet to visit. Most movies about Extraterrestrials have negative connotations. The Evil ones have done this so that we will be afraid of Extraterrestrials. Of course, all of us don't look like this."

"I don't care how crazy this sounds to y'all, one day y'all will find out it's true anyway, that in the center of your Planet, there is another world. There's subterranean pathways to different chambers

in the center of your Planet. The Pyramids are entrances there...out at the Antarctic is the entrance in...Elijah was taken up (2Kings 2:1) Enoch was translated into heaven (Genesis 5:24) it's throughout the scriptures. These stories that you have interpreted in the scriptures strictly as religious dogma because of the translations by the Christian Churches who had no knowledge of Extraterrestrials. They have turned this Spiritual Community of beings who have existed in other Galaxies into Gods or into Angels and gave them a bunch of names that didn't apply to them."

"There are many Extraterrestrials visiting from different Galaxies constantly. They're always here. They use clouds mostly as a cover. They're here at all times."

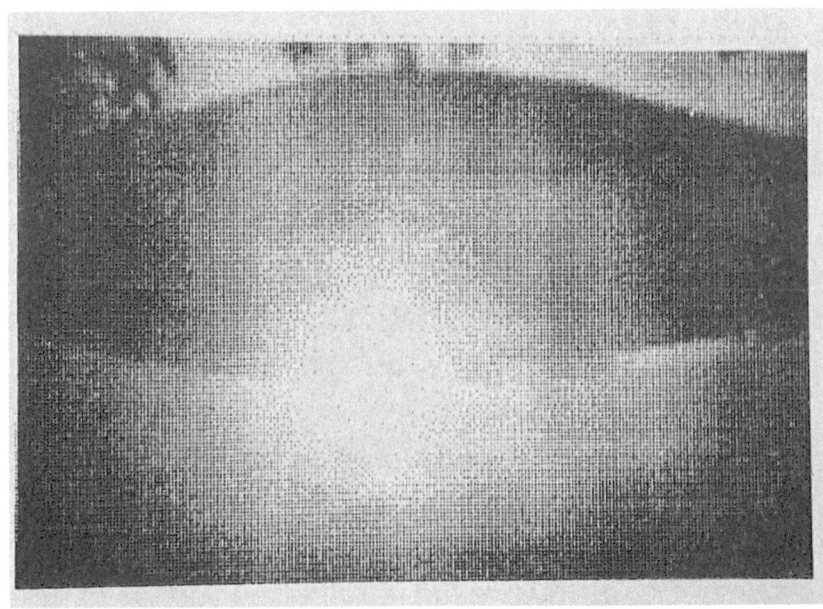

This is a picture of an Alien Craft taken
behind Dr. York's house in 1993 A.D.

"Extraterrestrials have been visiting this Planet for thousands of years. There are people who don't think the crafts are coming. But then they aren't supposed to because it's not for them anyway. Remember, Many are called, but few are chosen as it states in Matthew 22:14."

Question: Is there any way for them [Extraterrestrials] to come and get us?

Answer: *"First of all, You have to give up all this emotional stuff. You have to take care of your health, your body. You have to give up the laziness. Meaning, there are things about you that you need to correct before they come and get you, and if they are not corrected then when the Rizqiyians come they're going to pass you by. They have every right to, because you don't give them any reason not to. Look at the kind of people you are: Liars, Thieves, Worshippers of false gods, etc. Look at how you treat each other, you are jealous, envious and all just to live in the image of the beast. This is a part of The Spell. And as long as you are the type of person to harbor animosity and are always trying to get back at someone, you will never make it on the ship. And as long as you hold things against people, and are spiteful and revengeful, always trying to get back at someone, because of that you'll never make it on the ship. Yashua, Isa, Jesus of 2,000 years ago has taught us the way, we just won't follow."*

Luke 6:35

But love ye your enemies, and do good, and lend, hoping for nothing again; and your reward shall be great, and ye shall be the children of the Highest: for he is kind unto the unthankful and to the evil.

1. *Stop Smoking*
2. *Stop Drinking*
3. *Stop Whoring*
4. *Stop Adultery*
5. *Stop Cheating*
6. *Stop Stealing*
7. *Stop Cursing*
8. *Stop Lying*
9. *Stop Eating Unclean Foods*

"If you are not doing the right thing, and you have your little thing on the side, doing shady things, If you are wearing a ring with the Messiah on it, The ring will get through, However, you won't because your heart is not pure."

"I know you think I'm nuts; But in time, the whole World will know I am here, and who I really am."

In 2020 A.D. with all the outright injustice that has been broadcasted to the World concerning corrupt Officials, blatant disrespect of human life and criminals in the Justice System; it should not be beyond one's grasp that a group of small minded people in the Middle District of Georgia that belong to Law Enforcement and positions of power; would blatantly target, lie and try to destroy the life of a being such as Dr. York and his Community because of their own personal prejudices and fears.

However, this is the day and time where everything you want to know is at the tip of your fingers; The Information Age. You can do a internet search on the spot! Also, know that promoters of misinformation also upload on the "Net." Promoters of misinformation didn't just pop up with the advance of computers, they have always been around us doing their jobs! Take for instance "Wikipedia" which can be "edited by anyone at anytime" which is not a problem.

The problem comes in when editors are deceptive and inaccurate. Example: A Wikipedia search on Dr. York yields the following "York's case was reported as the largest prosecution for child molestation ever directed at a single person in the history of the United States, both in terms of number of victims and number of incidents."

Fact: Dr. York was charged with "transporting and traveling with minors for purposes of engaging in unlawful sexual activities and structuring cash transactions to evade currency reporting requirements" which the US Government alleged was "his pattern of racketeering activity"RICO).

[January 5, 2004 A.D. Case 5:02-CR-27-CAR]

Fact: There were no witnesses that said Dr. York ever travelled with a minor for the purpose of sex. On May 14, 2002 A.D. at The Detention Hearing, Defense Attorney Ed Garland for Dr. York asked FBI AGENT Jalaine Ward for the Prosecution the following question and I quote: *"Now, in connection with the travel for the purpose of having sex with a minor, do you have a witness who says that the purpose in the travel was to have the children have sex?"* FBI AGENT Jalaine Ward: **"No, not that says that, No."**

Now in terms of the number of victims, There were 49 testimonies listed for the Prosecution in Dr. York's case. Out of the 49 testimonies, 17 were FBI AGENTS, 2 were Putnam County Detectives, 1 Ex-Walmart Employee, 2 Expert Witness Pediatricians, 1 DFACS, 1 Expert Witness in the sexual victimization of children, 1 Wachovia Bank Employee, 1 Expert Witness for children, 1 Expert Witness Psychiatrist, 1 Expert Witness Nurse Practitioner, 1 Expert Witness Doctor, 1 Brunswick Postmaster, 1 UPS Worker, 10 Alleged Victims and 8 Witnesses.

Because the Courtroom was closed and the Trial Transcripts were sealed: The unknowing believe these were 49 victims but as you see that's not true.

Fact: There were 8 listed alleged victims in the indictment that the Government **never** presented. However, The Defense presented The Prosecution's ALLEGED VICTIMS who said they were NEVER sexually assaulted or sexually abused in any form or fashion by Dr. York.

Fact: Dr. York was accused of 11,568 acts of sexual assault from 1993 A.D. - 2001 A.D. That's 1,446 times a year, 121 times per month and not one alleged victim could identify any type marks, tattoos or scars on Dr. York's body.

Fact: There was no Pictures of Dr. York molesting children. There was no Videotapes of Dr. York molesting children. There were no

Photographs of Dr. York in the nude. There were no Photographs or Videos of Dr. York in any sexually compromising position with children. There was no Audio of Dr. York engaging in any type of vulgar or sexually explicit conversation with children. There was no Audio or Videotape statements of the Alleged Victims being interviewed by Law Enforcement Officials saying Dr. York ever molested them. Law Enforcement decided to not Audio or Video record their interviews with the Alleged Victims.

Fact: From 1970 A.D. -2002 A.D. There were over 1,000 children and Families who have come in and out the Community and interacted with Dr. York and not 1 Police Report has ever been filed of any child sexual abuse or assault against Dr. York. From 1970 A.D. - 2002 A.D. Never has there ever been a Medical Record of any child going to the Emergency Room or Doctor because of any wrong-doing or abuse by Dr. York.

Fact: The Prosecution's Key Witness RECANTED her False Trial Testimony in a Recorded Video as well as a Sworn Written Affidavit where she stated all of the allegations against Dr. York were all lies and how she was pressured by Law Enforcement to testify falsely against Dr. York.

Fact: Sworn Affidavits of the Alleged Victims exist where they deny ever being molested by Dr. York stating that FBI Threats led to their false Testimonies.

My point in stating the aforementioned is to say just because it appears on Wikipedia doesn't mean that it's false but it ALSO doesn't mean that's it true.

In a personal card from Dr. York to me while **TEMPORARILY** imprisoned at The Administrative Maximum Facility ADMAX in Florence, Colorado dated May 14, 2007 he said and I quote **"But from this I learnt so much about humans who stand next to you, smile at you, eat at your table, then stab you in the back."**

Oh...last but not least of this foreword. The words which The Man Of Miracles In This Day And Time wrote to me in that same very card which spoke the loudest were, "**Look at the Weather, Look at the fires, none control that save the heavens. I WILL WALK FREE SOON, WHY? BECAUSE I'M ON THE SIDE OF HEAVEN AND THE CHILDREN OF THE DEVIL, SATAN CAN ONLY TEST US.**"

DEDICATION

To all wrongly accused, wrongly convicted and wrongly imprisoned, may you be exonerated physically, mentally, emotionally and spiritually. Hold on to the rope of the Most High and let the miracle pull you through the muck and mire to your freedom. The Blessed Holy Mother Mary of Malachi.

GRATITUDE

First and foremost All gratitude is given to The Most High, The Most High The Highest. Next I'd like give thanks to my beloved consort Magnolia Madden for all her support and Amazingness throughout the years, My brother Rodney Madden for believing in me to support and help me so many times. My Mother Angela for all her love and everything I can't repay her for, My brother Vincent Long Jr. for protecting me in my youth and being there and last but not least My Father Noble Vincent Edward Long Sr. for reading Dr. York's books to us as children and driving evil and foolishness away from us with the rod of correction.

INTRODUCTION

"The government of America knows that whenever a people have been oppressed and suppressed and denied basic rights, freedom, justice and equality which are the essentials of life; They know that the longer we are deprived, the greater will be the leader that comes to answer that deprivation. So, they were watching to see who that leader was. They were looking for The Messiah, just like Pharaoh was looking for the birth of a deliverer and just like Herod was looking for the Messiah. They heard **Malachi York**; *They heard a brilliant Black Brother. They saw him building a small Nation here in Georgia. Is he the Messiah? Trumped up charges, break up his movement, put brother in Jail...Watch for the leader who is gaining strength, popularity, power, influence; Then if you can bring him into Court, fine! If you can't, find a way to trump up charges, FIND A WAY TO KILL HIM, FIND A WAY TO KILL HIM!* ~ **Minister Louis Farrakhan**

"We (Aiders of The Most High) do accept the duty to clean up the filth (Lies told about Dr. York) made by the west (United States) and it's fools in flesh (Black & White Devils)" ~ **Ansaarullah**

There is not an Introduction that can be tailor made for Dr. York because the size of his works are too big to fit, however, what we will do is perform a necessary exorcism on the demonization of Dr. York's character by way of the Media and slanderers. "**The Time Is Now**" Dr. York was born June 26, 1945 A.D. of Sudanese and Native American birth on the same day the charter of the United Nations was signed and serving a very similar purpose; maintaining and establishing peace among different cultures and nationalities by uniting different peoples on the basis of facts regardless of race, religion and language in worldwide peaceful community. Like the United Nations building headquartered in New York; The headquarters of Dr. York's movement was and is in New York, Brooklyn.

Dr. Malachi Z. York is a teacher, linguist, musician and author of the most dynamic books (**500 plus**) written in history. Some of which have been translated in other languages, with an equal amount of lectures covering topics such as Theology, Scriptures & Spiritual writings, Biographies of great Nubian Leaders, Customs and Traditions, Pagan Holidays, Science, UFOs & Extraterrestrials, Islaamic Studies, Comparative Religious Studies, History as well as Ancient Egyptian & Sumerian History and The True Story of The Messiah Jesus just to name a few.

In the beginning of Dr. York's mission which was 1970 A.D. he established the Ansaarullah Community a.k.a. The Nubian Islaamic Hebrew Mission which focused on building up the self-esteem of Nubians who have been exploited by Pale Arabs and Europeans who created a white concept of the Holy Men and Women of the Scriptures and all the important people throughout history that were depicted as pale with straight hair which in turn gave Nubians an inferiority complex. Dr. York erased that feeling of inferiority by creating images Nubians can relate and look up to. In the heart of Brooklyn, New York, The Ansaarullah Community a.k.a. The Nubian Islaamic Hebrew Mission raised the children in a clean peaceful relaxing environment guarded against drugs, disease and the corruption that plagues so many of our communities here in America.

The prime of Dr. York's life was spent and dedicated to saving the youth from self-destructive behavior such as dark Parties, Gangs, rowdy surroundings, Books and Tapes with lots of lust and killing, songs that create discontent, music that gives rise to negative thoughts and music and television programs centered on violence and Sensuality.

From 1970 A.D. - 2002 A.D. (Dr. York's arrest) Dr. York dedicated his time and energies toward the proper development of 1) The Minds of the youth through Right Knowledge, Truth and Facts, 2) The Bodies of the youth through proper Diet & Exercise and 3) The Souls of the youth through proper prayer and positive meditation. For over 30 years Dr. York allowed himself to be questioned in an open forum by people from all walks of life and schools of thought which have even become Debates & Discussion books as well as Question & Answer Classes in audio and video format that have been published in different languages so that everyone can receive the facts and truth.

Being fluent in the classical Arabic language Dr. York translated the Quran from Arabic into English, translated the Torah and The Psalms from the Ancient Aramic Hebrew into English as well as translating and explaining The Book of Revelation from the Arabic and the ancient Greek. Dr. York republished and revised The Holy Koran Circle Seven of The Moorish Americans under Noble Drew Ali also doing an in-depth study of the teachings of the Nation of Islam and the Honorable Elijah Muhammad which led him to the 5 percent Nation of Gods and Goddesses where Dr. York collected Data and published The Problem Book - their interpretation of the English Class Lessons of the Nation of Islam.

Blending in with each of the religions most interesting to his people, Dr. York lived and practiced as one of them in order to reveal the misconceptions of those doctrines that have plagued and diseased the minds of people and replacing misinformation, misinterpretations and mistranslations with facts. In January of 1993 A.D. Dr. Malachi Z. York moved from upstate New York and became a resident of Putnam County Georgia. The organization once known as the Nubian Islaamic Hebrews - Ansaarullah Community now became known as The Holy Tabernacle Ministries - A congregation of non- racial, unbiased people working for the upliftment of humanity. Being that the Southern States were neglected for years, The Holy Tabernacle Ministries (H.T.M.) key criteria was to make a concentrated effort to spread the truth throughout the South and every part of the world.

Prior to Dr. York moving down to Georgia he lived on a Shushoni Nubian Native American tribe reservation in the Catskill Mountains of upstate New York known as the New Foundation where he was and is known as "**Black Eagle**" identifying with his Native American culture. While identifying and linking with the Yamassee (Nubian Native Americans) Dr. York acquired 476 acres of Land in Eatonton, Georgia approximately 15 minutes away from Rock Eagle Mound - an ancient landmark built by the Yamassee tribe of Mound builders. Only 19 of the 476 acres were able to get developed due to zoning and minor building violations cited by local law enforcement due to their fear of Dr. York's community and influence in rural Georgia. The Land of the community was being styled into an Egyptian theme park that drew thousands of people each year during the annual "**Family Day**" gatherings held during the week of June 26 and lasting four to seven days where people from all over the world gathered in Love & Unity to enjoy different types of cultural music, different foods, sport tournaments and to hear the different stories about Dr. York's birth, the birth of the Tabernacle and the many metamorphosis of it.

There have been a host of great Nubian Leaders who have sprouted forth during the 19th and 20th Century that contributed to the upliftment of Nubians in the Wilderness of North America and abroad but there has not been 1 who has been gifted with as many talents as Dr. Malachi Z. York; A Singer, Musician, Music writer & Producer, Recording Artist, Dynamic Speaker, Entrepreneur, Healer, Community Organizer, Electrician, Tailor, Scientist, Reverend, Rabbi and Imaam of the highest spiritual caliber. It is safe to say that Dr. York is a rare occurrence.

However spiritually endowed or extraordinary the being Dr. Malachi Z. York is, he is not free from the persecution and opposition by adverse forces who are hell-bent on preventing the rise of a Messiah who could unify and raise the consciousness of the planet. Never claiming to be a Prophet, yet gifted with the ability to prophecy; Dr. York in a battle with the racism of Putnam County Planning and Zoning Board and Local Law Enforcement officials who prevented Nuwaupians from growing and flourishing in rural Georgia; said while on the Yamassee Native Americans tribal Land in Eatonton, Georgia in front of crowds of people, "If I was a Whiteman teaching...they'd have me in Universities giving me honorary degrees...but I'm black, they want to keep me hidden in prison under a dungeon if they can do it, ya hear me?! Cause they know I am their worst nightmare. In the Planet Of The Apes, I'm the monkey that could talk. They want to shut me up because wherever I go this happens (uniting the masses)."

In January 1993 when Dr. Malachi Z. York moved down to Putnam County from the Catskill Mountains in Upstate New York and acquired 476 acres of land in Eatonton Georgia. Some tribal members came down before Dr. York and some came after him. People began to wonder who this group of people were, why were they here and where did they come from. To address the concerns of the town's people, Newsletters and Leaflets were published and distributed by the Nuwaupians that addressed the fears that sprung up from rumors, insecurities and ignorance.

One such book that came out in 1994 was The Holy Tabernacle Family Guide authored by Dr. Malachi Z. York which gave details on who and what Dr. Malachi Z. York and his community are about and I quote, "*We accept as fact that no one race of people is better than the other. In fact no one wins the race in racism. We are a worldwide human movement for the survival, expansion and advancement of the human race who strives to unite all human peoples of the world on the basis of facts regardless of race, creed or language in a worldwide community. Respect the laws of the Government in which you live. Don't join any organization that is racist or any religious groups or organization that teaches hate.*" The Media in the Middle District of Georgia avoided quoting Dr. Malachi Z. York and his teachings. Instead, Nuwaupians were first targeted as a black supremacist compound and cult. The press in Middle Georgia has saturated the media with negative news coverage about Dr. Malachi Z. York and Nuwaupians; Thus an accurate history and knowledge of Dr. York and Nuwaupians is necessary in order to set the record straight and let the truth be told.

For 3 years there were no complaints or problems with the town's people or local officials. Then in 1997 A.D. Howard Richard Sills was elected Sheriff of Putnam County, Georgia and from this point on Nuwaupians found themselves involved in civil case after civil case regarding building and zoning violations. The big debut for Nuwaupians happened on March 3, 1998 A.D. when Fox 5 aired an interview they did with a former member of the Holy Tabernacle Ministries during which, they were "supposedly" informed that alcohol was being sold out of Rameses Social Club which was on the 476 acre land of the Nuwaupians. This is where the trouble started. The news report that aired on March 3, 1998 A.D. is what prompted Sheriff Sills to come out to the land on 404 Shady Dale Rd, Eatonton, Georgia with Jerome Dean Adams - Building Inspector who always gave Nuwaupians the run around for any requirements of building plans, and was always quick to reject them.

On March 18, 1998 A.D. the Fire Marshal of the safety fire division in Atlanta was "prompted" by the news report to inspect Rameses Social Club which resulted in 19 safety violations which Nuwaupians had no objection to correcting. Sheriff Sills blocked Rameses Social Club from being reopened for up to 5 months. Another strange thing was the former member who appeared with Doug Richards on March 3, 1998 A.D. terminated his membership immediately after the interview, and the kicker is; nowhere during the interview did the former member say Rameses Social Club sold alcohol. The plot thickens...

Rameses Social Club which was used for a diner as well as a lecture hall for members was registered with the State of Georgia as a Social Club. Yet Rob Peecher wrote an article in the Eatonton Messenger entitled "**Night club Trial Resumes today**" dated April 16, 1998 A.D. to imply that alcohol was sold. Rob Peecher also wrote an article dated April 23, 1998 A.D. entitled "**Judge fines $45, 750** in Night club zoning trial." Note that the fine amount was $45, 750. Yet according to the Macon Telegraph article dated July 28, 1998 A.D. by Cheryl Fincher entitled, "**Horton Company fined $5,000 for sludge spill.**" Horton Company could have been fined $50,000 a day after a bulldozer flattened a dairy lagoon dam allowing hundreds of pounds of cow manure to run off into a cove on Lake Oconee. But being that Horton took a proactive part to clean up the cove is what played a big part in the decision. Also to mention, Dudley Horton Jr. requested a rezoning for land on highway 441. When asked what he was going to put on it he answered, "None of your business." So why when Nuwaupians wanted to build an **Egypt of The West** on their land in Eatonton, Georgia; They had to give a comprehensive plan of what they were doing, what kind of building they wanted, What kind of houses and even the type of furniture? Could it be that Dr. York's freckles are too close?

Also to mention the ordinance fine imposed on Nuwaupians was against the law. According to Georgia Codes Annotated section 36-1- 20 states in part: Each such ordinance shall specify the maximum punishment which may be imposed for a violation of the ordinance; <u>and in no case shall the maximum punishment for the violation of such ordinance exceed a fine of $500 or imprisonment for 60 days or both</u>...

Another article which tarnished Dr. York and Nuwaupians in the eyes of the public was dated March 21, 1998 A.D. by Cheryl Fincher of the Macon Telegraph entitled, "**Putnam Cult charged with having illegal Nightclub**" called Nuwaupians a cult as opposed to a fraternal order working for the upliftment of humanity as expressed in Leaflets written by Nuwaupians such as "Welcome to the Holy Tabernacle Ministries where the uplifting of all humanity is our goal" "Who and what is the Holy Tabernacle Ministries?" "What our purpose is" "Fear of the unknown" and "They try to destroy things they don't understand." Further damage to Dr. York and the Nuwaupian Community was done by Cheryl Fincher's article in the Macon Telegraph entitled, "**Sheriff Padlocks Putnam group's Dance Club**" where the Nuwaupian Community was called a compound. A compound is defined as *a building or buildings especially a residence or group of residences set off and enclosed by a barrier. An enclosed area used for confining prisoners of war.* There were no barriers that enclosed the 476 acres of Land called "Tama-Re Egypt of The West." There was an Egyptian Pylon or "Entrance Way" with a security guard that monitored and controlled the flow of traffic.

The Nuwaupian Security force was a necessity because on different occasions in the past the town's authorities have shown that they were no help. Nuwaupians have had hate mongers passing by the community flashing lights, shooting and shouting obscenities. When reported to the authorities there was no response. So the need for Nuwaupians own security force came about. The security force was registered under Max International Inc. The public is only being told one side of the story. To further infer that **Egypt of The West** aka **Tama-Re** was a compound and not open to the public, another article written by Cheryl Fincher entitled "**Putnam Group wants to build Theme Park**" dated June 13, 1998 A.D. states in part "members who along with their guests would be eligible to use the proposed park [Tama-RE]" The insinuation here is that guest would have to be accompanied by members to visit Tama-Re. This is false because tourists from all over Georgia would come out daily. Thousands would come out for *Family Day*, thus it was not for members only.

Another article that emphasized negative points about Dr. Malachi Z. York and Nuwaupians was "**Nuwaupians Draw Community Attention**" by Jena Frazier dated May 9-11, 1998 A.D. where it says in part, "*yet others insist the order - a fanatical cult in need of close scrutiny.*" And Putnam County Sheriff Sills comment, "*Their publications are certainly similar to things like Heaven's Gate.*" The question that should come up is what has Dr. York and Nuwaupians said or done that made them Fanatical. And Secondly, "Heaven's Gate" unlike Nuwaupians had no public literature in distribution. Dr. York's literature has traveled around the world. How many reports/newspaper articles of Dr. York's literature being responsible or even influencing suicide have or can be referenced??? Yet, multiple unfounded media references abound. There is nothing in Dr. York's teachings that suggests that suicide is a means to salvation. Another participant to the demonization of Dr. York and Nuwaupians was a reporter by the name of Johnathan Burns of the *Macon Telegraph* in his articles entitled "**Nuwaupians Just do things different, Putnam Group Sheriff Near Agreement**" &" **Putnam Group will stay out of Club until Zoning in Line**" dated May 12, 1998 A.D. Johnathan Burns compares Nuwaupians to the Branch Davidians in Waco, Texas & David Koresh by saying, "*this is the post-Waco world after all.*" David Koresh and the branch Davidians were one group of people isolated in one place - Waco, Texas. Nuwaupians are worldwide, there's a difference. **Fact:** Rameses Social Club already had the electricity shut- off on April 20, 1998 A.D. by Sheriff Sills, Jerome Dean Adams (building inspector) and the Tri County EMC, by the order of Judge Sylvia Hoskins. **Fact:** On May 6, 1998 A.D., 6 days prior, Sheriff Sills and deputies from two counties invaded **Tama-Re - Egypt of The West** to change the locks on Rameses Social Club. Now, if the electricity was off and the locks were changed, how and why would Nuwaupians be using and going into Rameses Social Club?

As the injustice against Nuwaupians and Dr. York became apparent, certain reporters began writing factual articles in Nuwaupian's favor. The first example was an article dated May 7, 1998 A.D. by Matthew Willet of the Union Recorder entitled "**Sills Files Suit to close Club without support of County Commissioners**" where it says in part, "*We've got to be fair about it. We can't go around condemning people because we don't like them. You've got to be fair.*" Another favorable article for Nuwaupians and Dr. York was written by Don Schanche Jr of the Union Recorder dated May 8, 1998 A.D. entitled "*Griffin Concerned about overreaction to Nuwaupians*" Senator Griffin criticized Sheriff Sills for raiding Nuwaupian's Land. Senator Griffin "questioned why Sills needed such a strong show of force to change a lock on a door." Senator Griffin said, "*I was concerned about Nuwaupians being treated fairly* *and equally and that's the way everyone in that county [Putnam] and in this country should be treated, Fair and Equal."*

Nuwaupians went back to the Planning and Zoning Board and requested to rezone a 161 acre plot from Agricultural to Commercial which would allow Rameses Social Club to exist without violations. Some of the features that were planned to be built on Tama-Re were: Convenience Stores, Restaurants, Lodgings, a First-Aid Center, a Picnic Ground, and a Library to name a few. The Planning and Zoning Commission was to review the request on July 9, 1998 A.D. Come July 9, 1998 A.D. the request was postponed because the aerial survey was not sufficient for the Planning and Zoning Board, thus a second survey was requested by them. A special meeting was promised by the Board to vote in two weeks. The survey was not able to get done in two weeks, so a meeting was scheduled for August 6, 1998 A.D. Nuwaupian's rezoning request was postponed again because The Planning and Zoning Board members asked for a study of an impact of how Nuwaupian's Egyptian Theme Park would affect the Eatonton Community. This is the kind of run-around Nuwaupians faced with the Planning and Zoning Board.

Funny thing is a sludge and manure spill caused by Horton Homes that ended up in Oconee Lake wasn't in the news until after the incident was taken care of. It never made front page news. Isn't the water supply of Putnam County more important than a Social Club that's padlocked with no electricity? So how is it that Nuwaupians made the front cover of the newspapers in Atlanta, Savannah and Augusta, especially when Sheriff Sills said he could care less about what Nuwaupians are doing because they're not that important? The reality is that Nuwaupians are that important and they were and are breaking a stereotype. Rameses Social Club was open and free of drug involvement, crimes and robberies etc. Could it be that Dr. York and Nuwaupians would have been putting a person out of business who needed crimes to stay in business???

I.D. Channel - People Magazine - Investigates Cults - Factual Rebuttal to the Slander

On July 9, 2018 A.D. (Investigation Discovery) I.D. Channel aired episode 6 **People Magazine Investigates Cults: The United Nuwaubian Nation Of Moors**. During this airing there were fictitious accounts and lies that were broadcast which will be addressed with facts herein. Every single statement will not be addressed as it will be a waste of time and effort however Dr. Malachi Z. York's name will be cleared and you will have the facts of his innocence.

Christine Pelisek [pictured across] - **Senior writer for People Magazine** said, "When Dwight York started he was involved with the Black Panthers movement, The Nation Of Islam."

Fact - First of all, let's address the name "Dwight" that is unnecessarily attributed to Dr. Malachi Z. York too often. "Dwight" is Dr. York's nickname that was given to him by his mother's family because of their refusal to recognize his Arabic name "Isa" at birth. Thus, the acquisition of the American name

Dwight York. What makes the use of "Dwight" such a mockery and ridicule is that "Dwight York" cannot be found as the author of over 400 books and 100s of lectures covering such subjects as "The true story of the Messiah Jesus, Comparative Religious studies, History, Science, Spiritual Writings, Customs and Traditions, UFOs and Extraterrestrials Ancient Egyptian as well as Sumerian History" just to name a few; **Malachi York** can be found as such. So a "bogus" name is kept out in the public and listed in the BOP.gov (Bureau of Prisons) under the misnomer Dwight D. York 17911-054 at ADMAX Florence Colorado to keep him trapped in the U.S. Prison system by U.S. Government Officials to hide the fact that Dr. York was appointed Consul General of Liberia Diplomat# 003828-04 on December 15, 1999

in the state of Atlanta, Georgia on a diplomatic assignment by then President Charles G. Taylor of Liberia. Being that everything nowadays is at the tip of our fingers with computers; if one were to enter a Google or YouTube search on "Malachi York" and see the amount of intellectual philanthropy he has devoted, it would paint a different picture than the "Dwight" York which has been painted by Mainstream Media. Second of all, Dr. Malachi Z. York aka Dr. York was never involved with the Black Panther movement or the Nation Of Islam. As Dr. Malachi Z. York taught, "During the 60s I was involved in the "Black Thing" like everybody else; but, I never belonged to any Black Panther, Nationalist or Marxist group." (Refer to **The Ansaar Cult Rebuttal to the Slanderers by Dr. York, 1989 A.D. p. 60**) As far as Dr. Malachi Z. York being involved with the Nation of Islam he said, "*I was never a student enrolled in the Nation Of Islam like many Sunni Muslims fabricate but I would be honored to follow a man as great as The Honorable Elijah Muhammad.*" (Refer to **Message to the Black Man, True Light tapes** *Newcomer's Classes given by Dr. York at the Hall of Knowledge in Brooklyn, New York*)

Narrator -"*In 1972 York's growing Congregation moves to Bushwick Brooklyn. His most loyal followers are invited to live in Communal housing where everyone is separated by gender and age. The children attend Nuwaubian School.*"

Fact - During the beginning stages of Dr. York's Community he drew many hypocrites, phonies, and people that were living wayward lives. They wanted to dress up, play African drums, listen to him speak but not work to clean their lives up and sacrifice for the future. Community living is something that takes place everywhere. You have Jewish Communities, Chinese Communities, Mormon Communities and Native American Reservations, to name a few that are based on their laws. Dr. York's community is allowed this same right to exist. Yes, people were separated according to their gender and age because when Dr. York first set up headquarters out of an Apartment building on 2525 Bedford Avenue in Brooklyn, New York in 1967 A.D. they were in the beginning stages of building. Community living wasn't established until 1970 A.D. This was the beginning of "communal housing." Dr. York's goal was to have everyone in the community to have their own apartments with their families living together but until that would fruition people were separated in brackets of ages as well as gender. The narrator says, "Children attend a Nuwaubian School." The question that people should ask is, "Hmmm, Dr. York had a School for the children?" There was no "Nuwaubian" school for the children. The word "Nuwaupu" as a science wasn't taught to the children until the 90s.

Ruby [pictured below] - *"I'm sitting by myself [Ruby is 14yrs old in a local beauty salon according to the narrator] and this brother comes in all dressed in white. He walks over to me and passes me this book. I read it from cover to cover; it struck that chord in me that was affected by racism."*

Fact - Ruby Garnett is a "Pen name" or Pseudonym meaning false name. *"Part of the reason why she uses a pen name is because there's a possibility of retribution for her coming out with her story against Malachi York"* (**Refer to I survived Living in a Cult - A true Story by Ruby Garnett, Blog talk radio, Letteschat host 6-20-2013 A.D.**) If there was a fear of retribution then why did Ruby show her face and not disguise her voice? Documentaries shadow people's faces and alter their voices upon request. Furthermore, she created a public Facebook profile with the name Ruby Garnett advertising her book "**Soul Sacrifice: One Story of Many**" and video footage advertising "People Magazine - Cults on I.D. channel. Anyone that joined the Ansaaru Allah Community had to fill out an application.

This application was kept on file as a record. Without a record of who she is or pictures of her living within the gates of the Ansaaru Allah Community; events can be fabricated as was done in *The Ansar Cult in America by Bilal Phillips, Tawheed Publications, 1988 A.D.*; when he (Bilal Phillips) interviewed ex-members of the community who left for various reasons which had nothing to do with wrong doing on Dr. York's behalf and the facts are telling us that history is repeating itself again. Inside of Bilal's book there was an accusation by a woman named Fatima Muhammad who claimed to be one of Dr. York's concubines (**The Ansar Cult in America by Bilal Phillips, Tawheed Publications, 1988 A.D., p.152**) However, after Dr. York found out about the false accusations he wrote **The Ansaar Cult Rebuttal to the Slanderers by Dr. York, 1989 A.D.** to refute the lies. The fact of the matter was that Fatima Muhammad was welcomed into the community and taken in as Dr. York's daughter with his wife as her guardian. Fatimah was carrying herself in a manner that Dr. York did not condone and made it known to Fatimah. She later got involved with a man from Trinidad, left to be with him and then Dr. York washed his hands of her. For those reasons Fatimah was bitter and later out of anger and resentment lied to Bilal Phillips and said she was Dr. York's concubine. The point is that if Fatimah's name had not been known, there would be no way to fact check her lies. There were multiple lies in Bilal books about Dr. York and the community by disgruntled ex-members who had their own personal reasons for leaving and none of it had to do with Dr. York doing anything other than building up broken people. Ruby Garnett has not allowed herself to be fact checked because she doesn't give the name she was known in the community nor the time stamp of her being in the community in the documentary. There's no factual point of reference for Ruby. There's no record of her in the community to give an eye into her character. Second of all, the book they showed was "**The Sacred Wisdom of Tehut**i" [pictured across] *by Dr. Malachi Z. York* which did not come out until circa 2000 A.D. It was the corrected version of the Kybalion. Dr. York's catalogue of books is well known. Ruby did not mention the name of the book in the documentary, however in her book "**Soul Sacrifice: One Story of Many**" on page 33 she does and I quote, "*Before I could respond, he [Ansaar brother dressed in white] gave me the very same book that the mysterious brother from the Hair Salon had given me 2 years before this....and in slow motion I took the book called <u>Ahmad, Jesus' Khalifat (Successor)</u>.* This book was deliberately not mentioned in the documentary because People Magazine and Ruby Garnett did not want to reveal that Dr. York teaches as the Bible and Quran teaches that The Prophet Muhammad 570 A.D. - 632 A.D. of Arabia was the successor to Jesus. It would open the door to the Community's core belief and the foundation of Dr. York's works from the beginning of his mission in 1970 A.D. until NOW which is <u>**"To prepare you for his [The Real Messiah] coming, It is a very great matter. There are so many lies mixed in with facts that people don't want to hear. But it must be done for The Messiah's sake."**</u> (Refer to **pg.**

150 The Holy Tabernacle Family Guide Book 1994 A.D. by Dr. Malachi Z. York) This is the consistent theme of Dr. York's Pamphlets of Peace, videos & audio tapes and teachings throughout the years. Prior to his May 8, 2002 A.D. arrest Dr. York said, "<u>Right Knowledge has always talked about Christ; you just wasn't looking hard enough. I haven't said nothing other than one day he's coming</u>

<u>back. Whether I was an Indian or Cowboy. You got the wrong teacher.</u> **What happened is, you read my doctrine the way you wanted amongst your friends and now you are confused.** <u>All you got to do is open up any book written by me and it gets into the Lord & Savior; whether you want to call him Jesus, Tammuz, whatever name makes you feel good, he's coming. If you miss him, it's your fault because I presented him to you for 30 years. 30 years y'all."</u> (Refer to "**Help Jesus Separate the Sheep from the Goat**" class given by Dr. Malachi Z. York)

However, Ruby does give a misinformed nutshell synopsis of the book in her own book on pg. 33 where she says, "*it happened to breakdown the fallacies of the Christian Religion. It broke down how Jesus could not have been a Caucasian or of European descent (which I already had doubts about), and how Christianity was used by* <u>*the white man (who he referred to as the blond-haired, blue-eyed devil*</u>*) to enslave our people.*" First of all, **NOWHERE** in the book **Ahmad, Jesus' Khalifat (Successor) Edition #147** does Dr. York refer to the white *man* as the <u>blond- haired, blue-eyed devil</u>. Not only does Ruby lie about what Dr. York said in the book but she evades summarizing what the theme of the book is about - The Prophet Muhammad (Ahmad) being The Comforter (John 15:26) the Khalifat (Successor) whose purpose was to testify of Jesus and to teach only what Jesus, Moses and Abraham (Quran 61:6) taught before him (Muhammad).

Ruby -"*walking down Bushwick Avenue you had the Brothers with boom boxes and the Rastas on the corner. Finally, as you get closer to that community (Ansaaru Allah Community) the whole scenery changed. I started seeing little children running around in the garbs, speaking another language I didn't understand. It felt safe, it felt positive, it felt magical. Wow, this is someone that looks like me and they're calling him a Prophet."*

Fact - Dr. York never claimed to be a Prophet. Next, everything else she said is true which is confirmed when **The New York Times** printed an article dated April 24, 1994 A.D. by Dennis Hevesi entitled, "**Muslims Leave Bushwick; The Neighbors Ask Why.**" *[Notice the Neighbors are asking "Why" and not saying "Thank God they're leaving"] The article says in part: "Their absence has profoundly changed the nature of the area along Bushwick Avenue between Willoughby and Dekalb Avenue, where they were an anchor of stability in an otherwise troubled neighborhood...There are many reasons the remaining residents wish the sect had not left...Michael Jimenez, 56 who has lived on Bushwick Avenue for 30 years said, the sect members" were good neighbors"...Sect members stood guard on every street corner around the clock, Mr. Jimenez said, "the crooks, the addicts, they would pass by here. They knew they weren't welcomed." The exodus, Mr. Jimenez said, has hurt the neighborhood. They worked hard, they had their morals, they were clean. Now that buildings across the street has had three fires, it would be better if they were still here."* Things that make you go "How come I never heard this about Dr. York and Nuwaupians?"

Ruby - "Wow, this is someone that looks like me and they're calling him a Prophet."

Fact - Dr. York never called himself a prophet. Dr. York has taught countless times throughout the years "*I am not a prophet, just read my lips, I am not a Prophet.*" (**Refer to The Ansaar Cult Rebuttal to the Slanderers by Dr. York, 1989 A.D pg. 585**).

Niki [pictured below] - *He felt like he took our virginity, we're connected and loyal to him. I was born and raised and baptized Christian but when I was 5 my mom came across one of the books, she connected with that ideology.*

········· BIOGRAPHICAL REBUTTAL TO PEOPLE MAGAZINE ·········

Fact - Niki is short for "Nicole" Lopez who was also known as "Adah." "Niki" was a witness for the prosecution who was given immunity during Dr. York's 2004 Trial in Brunswick, Georgia.

"**Adrian Patrick** *(Defense Attorney for Dr. York) - Now, you have an immunity agreement; correct?*
Niki *(Nicole) - Yes.*
  [**January 8, 2004 A.D. Trial Testimony Case 5:02-CR-27-CAR**]

When a person is given immunity they are exempt from being prosecuted for crimes in exchange for their testimony. So, what was "Niki's" crime? Child molestation. However, Niki doesn't consider herself a child molester.

Adrian Patrick *(Defense Attorney for Dr. York) - But you are a child molester; correct?*
Niki *(Nicole) - I don't consider myself a child molester.*
Adrian Patrick - *You mentioned that you had sexual intercourse with Kuwsh; correct?*
Niki - *Yes*

Adrian Patrick - *And you did that on your own; correct?*
Niki - *Well, it wasn't entirely on my own...it wasn't until after I talked with Doc (Dr. York) that I had sex with him.*
Adrian Patrick - *Basically, you're blaming the defendant for molesting Kuwsh; correct?*
Niki - *I'm not blaming him. I'm basically saying that's how it went.*
   [January 8, 2004 A.D. Trial Testimony Case 5:02-CR-27-CAR]

Kuwsh Muhammad - Martinez who Niki admits to having sex with according to Kuwsh's own sister Farah Muhammad in her June 1, 2004 video where she reveals the conspiracy to bring Dr. York down with allegations of child molestation states the following.

Farah - *"I know all of the alleged victims personally. They lived at my house. When most of the girls left the land they came to live at my father's house. <u>Adah Nicole Lopez (Niki)</u>; she moved there and <u>that struck me as odd</u> because when she left, her mother [Barbara Noel] was already off the land. She could've lived with her mother. She could've lived with her father as well because he wasn't even involved with the organization. Ironically, he didn't live that far from my house. He lived about 15 minutes away. It struck me as odd that she moved there; then again it didn't, because <u>I know that she was involved with my brother (Kuwsh). She (Niki) was molesting my brother beginning when he was about 13 or 14.</u> He was living on the land at the time. I think <u>she was like 23 and once I remembered that, I was like ok, that's why she's here.</u>"*
   [Farah Muhammad June 1, 2004 Eyewitness conspiracy video]

Farah Muhammad's testimony as an eyewitness to the conspiracy to bring Dr. York down was blocked by the Trial Judge C. Ashley Royal during Dr. York's 2004 trial.

Niki being a child molester was also confirmed by the Prosecution's Key witness **Habiba "Abigail" Washington's Recant Video dated April 18, 2004 A.D.** where "Abigail" says, *"Nicole (Niki) was in love with one of the younger boys. And so Jacob (Dr.*

York's estranged son, which will be elaborated on later) knew that if they (FBI) found out that about Nicole; Nicole would be so afraid that she could be <u>prosecuted</u> with that, she would also be compelled to tell a story about his father because she didn't want to be <u>incriminated</u> for whatever feeling she had."

Jess Cagle [pictured on next page] - **Editor in Chief People Magazine** - *"If you move into York's commune he provides you with shelter and food and work but in return for what he gives you, he demands complete control over every aspect of your life, right down to which male follower you're going to marry and have children with."*

Fact - This is an obvious exaggeration which goes to show that Jess Cagle has been misinformed and did not do his research with the intent of dealing with facts in this documentary; but focused instead on sensationalism. How can Dr. York demand complete control over every aspect of people's lives when people VOLUNTARILY leave?

Leaving or walking away from the community is an *"aspect of your life"* If Dr. York *"demands complete control"* then why wasn't this aspect of their lives controlled by Dr. York for those who VOLUNTARILY left? A case in point is the "Green Room" of the Ansaaru Allah Community. The brothers of the community had a meeting and Dr. York asked for their suggestions (does that sound like *"complete control"*). A brother by the name of Allen Redd "Saadiyq" ex-member of the community proposed the idea to have a place where husbands and wives could frequent when the community was in the beginning stages of building. Thus, the "Green Room" was initiated and not by Dr. York's demand.

Jess Cagle - *right down to which male follower you're going to marry and have children with."*

Fact - The Ansaaru Allah Community was an Islaamic Community linked to the Ansaars of Sudan with the same customs and laws. Marriages here in America are not as carefully planned as they are in other societies, whereas in Islaamic societies it is stricter. For instance elaborate weddings in the Ansaaru Allah Community were reserved for virgins only and non-virgins were not entitled to such a wedding. This is not "complete control" it's called The Islaamic (Peaceful) way of life.

Narrator - *As for himself York is a proud polygamist, in defense and defends the practice by loosely reciting passages in the Koran.*

Fact - "Proud Polygamist?" Let's analyze this statement. Dr. York during the establishment of The Ansaaru Allah Community fasted the month of Ramadan (2:185) and defended the practice by reciting passages in the Qur'aan, yet he never claimed to be a proud Ramadan- ist. Dr. York during the time also performed the obligatory Prayers (Qur'aan 30:16) and defended the practice by reciting passages in the Qur'aan, yet he never claimed to be a proud Salaat-ist or Prayer-ist. It must be established here that whenever someone asked Dr. York if he is a Muslim he would say and I quote <u>"Insofar as the meaning of the word Muslim, which is "**one who is of peace**" because I was of peace. I had absolutely nothing to do with East Arabs and have always said they were hypocrites, Our</u>

Community was like none other, Not even the Ansaars of Sudan. We were not even like them." As a Muslim (One who is of peace) in the Ansaaruallah (Qur'aan 61:14) Community where they are told to live as one community (Qur'aan 3:103) having up to 4 wives if you feel you can treat them fairly, but if not have just 1 (Qur'aan 4:3); is a part of the culture of Al Islaam (The Peaceful Way of Life). "Proud Polygamist" is a just another stone thrown by the hands of sensationalist media. Dr. York has never claimed to be such. Just like the term "Prophet" which others attributed to him.

Christine Pelisek - *"Polygamy isn't a red flag for York's followers because York was the Savior. Everyone wanted to have a relationship with York."*

Fact - This is just ridiculous because it implies that Savior's are sought after for sex by their followers, really Christine? First of all, Dr. York's own family from his Mother (Peace & Blessings Be Upon Her), Sister and children follow Dr. York. Does this mean that they too "wanted to have a relationship [Sexual] with Dr. York?" There are countless testimonials from followers of Dr. York who express their gratitude and love they have for Dr. York because of him touching their hearts and minds with his teachings and changing their lives for the better. Does this mean that they *"wanted to have a "relationship" with York?"* as you are insinuating? Also, If you refer to the **FBI COINTELPRO memo dated March 4, 1968**, Dr. King, Malcolm X and The Honorable Elijah Muhammad were all listed as "Saviors" aka Black Messiahs. Besides the United States Government viewing these men as "Saviors"; Multitudes of Men and Women to this day see them as the same, but it does not mean they seek to have the relationship you're trying to affix to a "Savior."

Jess Cagle - *"At this point York is having sex with dozens and dozens of women. Some of these women were the other brother's wives and they were considered York's concubines. But his favorites were invited to join the Family as one of his wives. If you were a woman in the*

Cult and you were invited to York's personal harem, it was considered the greatest gift."

Fact - The reason for these sex accusations is because the first step in eliminating a Nubian Leader of influence is to assassinate their character by planting rumors and thoughts of doubt in the minds and hearts of their followers. Whether you believe in a messiah coming or not; The United States Government is well aware of a messiah rising and have preventative measures in place aimed at anyone who can unify and influence a mass majority of people. People Magazine's theme is that Dr. York is this sex crazed fanatic with an uncontrollable sexual appetite; Yet in 1974 A.D. when the community first moved into 743 Bushwick Avenue, Brooklyn, New York; Dr. York did not have sex for a year and a half until renovation was finished in and out of the building. That's why the "Green Room" was established by and for those who didn't have the sexual restraint Dr. York had. Proof of this is in the fact that Jacob York who is Dr. York's son was born July 11, 1973 A.D. which is a year before Dr. York and the community moved in Building 743 in the year 1974 A.D. Dr. York did not have any children until two years later in 1975 A.D. when his daughter Zaynab was born. **Jess Cagle** says *"Some of these women were <u>the other brother's wives and they were considered York's concubines</u>."* This is to imply that the "brothers," their "wives" and Dr. York had no morals. Jess Cagle, you have to look at who is feeding you information and not what information they are feeding you. You are looking at Dr. York through the eyes of a character such as Niki. Through the eyes of a child molester an innocent man can appear as such. Niki allowed her younger sister Amala "Amanda" Noel (alleged victim) who was a minor at the time to bring alcohol to a party on the land while their mother Barbara Noel was in the same house. Dr. York was not even on the land at the time according to Dr. York's 2004 Trial below:

Adrian Patrick *(Defense Attorney for Dr. York) - Now, do you recall an incident where a lot of people had left the land; the defendant*

(Dr. York) wasn't at the land? I think people were going to a parade somewhere where there was a party. Do you recall this?

Niki - *Yes*
Adrian Patrick - *And you organized that party correct; correct?*
Niki - *No*
Adrian Patrick - *But let me be clear about one thing. The defendant (Dr. York) was no-where around; correct?*
Niki - *No, he was not.*
Adrian Patrick - *The defendant (Dr. York) had nothing to do with the party; correct?*
Niki - *No*
Adrian Patrick - *But you're aware that -- are you aware your sister said that they (Krystal "Beluwra" Hardin - alleged victim) broke into the house.*
Niki - *Yeah...I'm aware that she took alcohol from somewhere.*
Adrian Patrick - *Your sister was a minor; right?*
Niki - *Yes*
Adrian Patrick - *And she had alcohol; correct?*
Niki - *Yes*
Adrian Patrick - *And you allowed her to bring that alcohol to that party; correct?*
Niki - *Yeah. She brought it, yeah.*
Adrian Patrick - *Your mother was in that house; correct?*
Niki - *Yeah. She was sleep in the other room.*
   [January 8, 2004 A.D. Trial Testimony Case 5:02-CR-27-CAR]

Jess Cagle says - *But his favorites were invited to join the Family as one of his wives.*

Fact - Everyone in the community was and is family. Proof of this is in the fact that every week "family meetings" were held every week where all inside the community would discuss problems as well as the community's goals for the future. Because of Dr. York's intelligence, works, wealth, high moral character and influence; of course women would be attracted to him, as many women would be to any man with such a reputation. Just because a woman was Dr. York's wife doesn't mean that women who were not, weren't treated as family; And some who were taken in by Dr. York and cared for by him as a father later claimed to be his "concubines" when in fact they were welcomed in his own home and cared for like a daughter as was Faatimah in the community who left and later slandered due to bitterness. [**Refer to The Ansaar Cult Rebuttal to the Slanderers p. 506, 1989 A.D, Dr. York.**]

Jess Cagle says - *If you were a woman in the Cult and you were invited to York's personal harem, it was considered the greatest gift."*

Fact - *"If you were a woman in the Cult."* The majority of the public doesn't know what a cult is except for the interpretation given by the Media which results in a concept of a Mass suicide group and images of David Koresh and the Branch Davidians, Marshall Applewhite and Heaven's Gate and Jim Jones of Jonestown, Guyana flashes in the mind. Dr. York taught when you call us a cult add the next three letters cult-u-r-e. The Ansaarullah Community is linked with a culture in Sudan that has been there for thousands of years. The long white robe or Jallabiya of Sudan, The marriage and Birth Ceremonies of Sudan as well as the classical Arabic language of Sudan and the Original Qur'aan which was taken and protected by Muhammad's true descendants in Sudan.

Jess Cagle says *"and you were invited to York's personal harem it was considered the greatest gift"*

Fact - This is more sensationalism. Harim is an Arabic word used for the female apartments in an Islaamic household. "it was considered the greatest gift." When you're misinformed ignorantly or deliberately it's hard to give a great man his due. Because of who Dr. York is as a Master Teacher some viewed it as a position of high status to be associated with Dr. York and would even lie and tell young children in the community that Dr. York was their father. In particular, Niki's own mother Barbara Noel lied to her children to make them think Dr. York was their father. The child that was lied to was David "Taariq" Noel the brother of Niki. (*Refer to David "Taariq" Noel's Trial Testimony below*)

Richard Moultrie *(Prosecuting Attorney) - Was there a time when you believed that Mr. York was actually your father?*
David "Taariq" Noel - *Yes*
Richard Moultrie - *How old were you when you realized he wasn't your father?*
David "Taariq" Noel - *I was in my teenage years - I found out in '99.*
Richard Moultrie - *How did you find out he (Dr. York) wasn't your father?* **David "Taariq" Noel** - *My mom told me.*
[January 9, 2004 A.D. Trial Testimony Case 5:02-CR-27-CAR]

Ruby Garnett - one of my really close friends came to me personally and she said, *"Why don't you join the family."*

Fact - According to a BlogTalkRadio interview entitled **I survived Living in a Cult - A true Story by Ruby Garnett, Blog talk radio, Letteschat host 6-20-2013 A.D.)**

I quote the hostess *"When you moved into the facility [Community] you were married."* Ruby does not deny nor refute that statement in her blog talk radio interview. So if you were married what made you want to pursue Imaam Isa (Dr. York)? How do we know that she wanted to pursue Dr. York? Because she says in the same Blog talk radio interview, *"So I got a job working in the office...a few of my friends said that's where you'll see Imaam Isa (Dr. York) walking around, so I said Oh, Okay."*
Ruby says in the BlogTalkRadio interview, *"I think I had been in there (Community) 2 years before I actually met him face to face."*

Wait a minute... Jess Cagle said earlier that "*At this point York is having sex with dozens and dozens of women. Some of these women were the other brother's wives.*"

So a new woman comes into the community and the sex fanatic that Dr. York is alleged to be; He doesn't meet this woman face to face until about 2 years?! If people would take the time to think they would see that these accusations against Dr. York are not adding up and don't make sense. Ruby reveals the motives about herself in the community on the BlogTalkRadio interview.

"*You get either picked to come there or you <u>strategize</u> a way to stay there and <u>kick everybody else out</u>... It was funny, it would be like, Ok, you need to go home or you know, he said you need to go home, <u>none of it was true half the times</u>, sometimes it was, sometimes, <u>a lot of times it wasn't</u>.*"

> **(Refer to I survived Living in a Cult - A true Story by Ruby Garnett, Blog talk radio, Letteschat host 6-20-2013 A.D.)**

So Ruby strategically lied a lot of times.

Hostess - "*What went wrong, what happened?*"
Ruby - "*The first time where I was actually disillusioned was when we moved, we were in Georgia...she was* **8 years old.**"
Hostess - "*And she told you, she came to you and told you that this leader had his private parts in her mouth.*"

> **(Refer to I survived Living in a Cult - A true Story by Ruby Garnett, Blog talk radio, Letteschat host 6-20-2013 A.D.)**

Here it seems that Ruby Garnett is disillusioned about her disillusions because in the (Investigation Discovery) I.D. People Magazine Investigates Cults documentary Ruby says, "*I saw one of my co-wives daughters, she was crying and she was hysterical. She was screaming in Arabic "Baba's!@#$% was in my mouth, Baba's!@#$% was in my mouth." **She was only 5.**"

Number 1. Was she 8 years old or 5 years old? **Number 2.** Earlier in the documentary Ruby says that Dr. York told her that he would take a 15 or 16 year old virgin minor and sodomize her in the back of the home. Ruby said she was terrified. Wouldn't that be your first disillusion being that you were terrified that Dr. York was sodomizing a virgin minor? Then again how terrified was Ruby being that she says she followed Dr. York to Georgia? Usually people run AWAY from a monster that terrifies them, not towards them. You have to ask yourself, how much of a Monster is Dr. York that people follow him after knowing he's such a Monster?

According to Ruby's BlogTalkRadio interview after the 5 or 8 year old girl tells her she's been molested Ruby says, "*I said you know what, I'm going to go say something but then I thought about it; Number 1. What am I going to say about this to him? Number 2. What can I do about it? Number 3. If he knows that I know, what then?*"

(Refer to I survived Living in a Cult - A true Story by Ruby Garnett, Blog talk radio, Letteschat host 6-20-2013 A.D.)

Ruby - *Number 1. What am I going to say about this to him?*

Fact - What sane person can witness a child say they were molested and do absolutely nothing?

Ruby - *Number 2. What can I do about it?*

Fact - This is how you know this alleged incident did not happen. This may be one of the most ignorant replies made in the history of BlogTalkRadio.

Ruby - *Number 3. If he knows that I know, what then?*"

Fact - This is not adding up because on the People Magazine - Cults documentary Ruby said that Dr. York told her that he was sodomizing a virgin minor. So Ruby allegedly knew already of minors being molested and Dr. York allegedly was aware that you knew of it because he told you as you allege. A liar ultimately reveals the truth they were trying to hide.

Ruby continues in her BlogTalkRadio and says, "*I thought about all these things because Uh, Nobody knew where I was...*"
Here's another lie Ruby tells because the Hostess said earlier, "*Your brother at one point was going to break you out, What finally made you leave?*"

Fact - If nobody knew where Ruby was then how was her brother going to break her out, if he didn't know where she was located? You have to know where a person is in order to break them out.

Ruby says in the blog talk radio interview that one of the reasons she didn't do or say anything at the time about the alleged 5 or 8 year old alleged molestation incident is because and I quote, "*I was the trouble-maker, I couldn't just go and talk to him...*"

Fact - Ruby did mention earlier that she strategically lied a lot. Refer to her BlogTalkRadio interview statement where she said, "*You get either picked to come there or you strategize a way to stay there and kick everybody else out... It was funny, it would be like, Ok, you need to go home or you know, he said you need to go home, none of it was true half the times, sometimes it was, sometimes, a lot of times it wasn't.*"

Niki - "*A little after I joined the community, my Mom became one of his wives. That meant I was one of his children and I looked up to him...that's my Dad.*" **Fact** - Niki's mom Barbara Noel as mentioned above while in the community in Georgia "Tama-Re" aka "The Land" while Dr. York was NOT present on "The Land" was in a separate room while teenagers were having a party drinking alcohol and engaged in sexual activities and Dr. York was NOT present. Not only did Barbara Noel's daughter "Niki" Nicole Adah Lopez" confirm this during trial but Barbara Noel's other daughter

Amala "Amanda" Noel during her trial testimony in the case of USA vs York where she is listed as an alleged victim also confirms it below.

Adrian Patrick - *"Do you recall the incident where everyone had gone to South Carolina marching in a parade, and you, Nicole (Niki) Lopez's sister Ida, Krystal Hardin, Kuwsh and others engaged in sexual activity?"*

Amala "Amanda" Noel - *"Where?"*
Adrian Patrick - *"Not exactly sure but it occurred correct?"*
Amala "Amanda" Noel - *"I remember in 103 there was a party, but I was on my period so I didn't do anything."*
Adrian Patrick - *"But you remember a lot of people had left the land; correct?"*
Amala "Amanda" Noel - *"Yes"*
Adrian Patrick - *"And the defendant (Dr. York) was not present; correct?"*
Amala "Amanda" Noel - *"No"*
Adrian Patrick - *"And do you recall you and Krystal Hardin breaking into the main house and taking alcohol out of there?"*
Amala "Amanda" Noel - *"Yes"*
Adrian Patrick - *"You went into the main house; you didn't have permission; and y'all just stole alcohol; correct?"*
Amala "Amanda" Noel - *"Yes...my mother (Barbara Noel) was in the sewing room."*
Adrian Patrick - *"Your mother was at the party?"*
Amala "Amanda" Noel - *"No, she wasn't at the party."*
Adrian Patrick - *"She was in another building?"*
Amala "Amanda" Noel - *"Yeah -- no, she was in a separate room"*
Adrian Patrick - *"And some people were engaging in sexual activity; right?"*
Amala "Amanda" Noel - *"Yes"*
Adrian Patrick - **"Your mother was in the other room?"**

Amala "Amanda" Noel - *"Yes"*

[January 7, 2004 A.D. Trial Testimony Case 5:02-CR-27-CAR]

Niki's mom Barbara Noel who came into the community with her children was the type of person that would be in a separate room while minors were drinking alcohol and engaged in sexual activities. Niki's mom Barbara Noel also tried to bribe Dr. York 4 months after his arrest May 8, 2002 A.D. via an e-mail dated September 8, 2002 which read.

"Let Doc know that I need 10 money orders for $500.00 and they could be made out to me, for a donation, from different concerned members sent, to me at this address:
P.O. Box 3xxxxx
Decatur, GA 3xxxx-xxxx I NEED this by Sept 10th
This will show good faith on his part to honor his word that he will help me & the kids. Tell him it is in HIS best interest to help me now, maybe "we" could talk and agree on something for our mutual benefit. I expect a reply today from you, this way I know what I should do and plan for tomorrow. This is very important...this is very serious."

[Case 5:02-cr-00027-CAR Document 407-17 Filed 03/02/09]

Christine Pelisek - *"At this point, Dwight York has 30 wives and 100 children and some of the girls like Niki are starting to be treated differently than some of the other girls."*

Okay. Niki Lopez moved in the community when she was 11 which would be 1986 A.D. So from 1970 A.D. (when Dr. York received his calling) to 1986 A.D.; Dr. York had acquired 30 wives and 100 children according to Christine Pelisek who said "At this point." So that's 30 wives, 100 children in 16 years. Dr. York was arrested May 8, 2002 A.D. which would be 16 years from 1986 A.D. So another 16 years would have allowed Dr. York to acquire a total of 60 wives and 200 children assuming he had the same alleged stamina he had from 1970 A.D. to 1986 A.D. Okay. Now, this is not taking into account the alleged sex acts that Dr. York was accused of during his 2004 Federal Trial below:

Adrian Patrick - "All right. Also, there's another practical point I would like to make. I outlined the number of times that the witnesses alleged sex acts occurred. The question I have for you, "Is it physically possible?" Amanda Noel [alleged victim], we estimated, said that from '93 to about '95, about 2 to 3 times per week; '95 to 2001, about 1 to 2 times per week. So, we added all those up and came up with a total of 1,092 times that he (Dr. York) had sexual activity allegedly with Amanda Noel. Now, with [Niki] Nicole Adah Lopez, she stated from '93 to '95, virtually every day; from '95 to 2000, approximately 2 times per week. So, if you go each year and down to your total, it's 1,306 times. Now, Khalid Eddington, or Eddie, he alleged that from '93 to; 96, about 3 times per week, a total of 624 times. David Noel, from '93 to '95, he alleged 2 to 3 times per week; '95 to 2001, he alleged 3 to 4 times per week. That would mean that there were 1,768 times. Abdul Salaam Shilemoh LaRoche, he stated it was a total of about 9 times. Jin Hee...she stated about 1 time per week from '93 to '95; about 156 times. Atiyah Thomas, from '93 to 2001, total time would have been about 1,404 times. Sakinah Parham alleged from '93 to '99, 3 times per week; total 1,092 times from '93 to '99. Ebony Hill alleged from 1990 to 1997 2 to 3 times per week. The total would have been 1,248 times. Nicole Harden alleged from '93 to 2000 about a total of 4 times. Safa'a LaRoche basically stated, '96 to 2000, everyday; for a total of 1,825 times with Safa'a LaRoche. Kyrstal Harden alleged from '96 to 2000 3 to 4 times per week; total 1,040 times. The grand total of alleged sex acts from '93 to 2001 is 11,568 times; alleged sex acts per year 1,446 times; alleged sex acts per month 121 times."

[January 22, 2004 A.D. Trial Testimony Case 5:02-CR-27-CAR]

Now bear in mind these alleged sex acts did not include the alleged victims who didn't give a frequency of alleged acts to be added in. In other words some did not give a number of alleged sex acts per week to be added up, so it wasn't a part of the 11,568 total that was mentioned. Also, on top of all those alleged sex acts; Dr. York's alleged 30 wives and 100 children according to Christine Pelisek and 30 more wives and 100 more children according to the frequency of his alleged sexual appetite would also have to be taken into consideration. What's also interesting is that during the entire documentary "**People Magazine - Cults**"; not one time did anyone in the documentary mention the amount of books that Dr. York had written "At this time" which were 158 books "*At this time*" which was 1986 A.D., the listing of books written by Dr. York were:

1. Back to the beginning: The Book of Names
2. Why The Beard?
3. Was Christ Really Crucified?
4. Are The Scriptures Tampered with (Pt 1 & 2)?
5. Our Symbol
6. The Dog
7. Talisman
8. Yoruba
9. Science of Healing
10. Bilaal
11. Who was the Prophet Mustafa Muhammad Al Amin
12. Muslim Prayer Book, Vol. 1 & 2
13. Muhammad Ahmad Al Mahdi, The Only True Mahdi (Pt 1 & 2)
14. Hajj
15. Leviathan 666
16. Did the Hog come for Mankind?
17. The Lost Children of Mu and Atlantis
18. The Tribe of Israel is no more
19. Islaamic Poetry
20. The Paleman
21. Sons of Canaan
22. From Allah to Man
23. Men who dress in Women's clothes
24. Why the Nosering?

25. Is the Holy Qur'aan a product of man?
26. Hadiyth (Pt 1 & 2)
27. Fast of Ramadaan
28. Tribal Encyclopedia
29. Why Allah Should not be called God
30. Eternal Life after Death
31. Great African Kings
32. What is a Masjid?
33. Adam's Calendar
34. Thus said the Prophet
35. What's your Astrology sign brother?
36. The Muslim Man, Vol. 1
37. The Muslim Woman
38. Why do Muslim Women wear the veil?
39. Tajwiyd - The proper reading of the Qur'aan
40. Menstruation
41. The Holy Qur'aan, The Last Testament (Vol 1, 2, 3)
42. Islaamic Music
43. Science of the Pyramids
44. Polytheism: The worship of the Canaanites
45. Forgotten tribe of Kedar
46. Arabic: Mother of all languages
47. Islaamic Festivals and Ceremonies
48. Arabic made easy (Pt.1), Teach yourself Arabic (Pt.2)
49. Islaamic Marriage Ceremony and Polygamy
50. Christianity: The Political Religion
51. Thoughts of Muslim Women in Poetry
52. Islaamic Cookery
53. Dietary Laws of a Muslim
54. The Sex life of a Muslim (Pt.1)
55. Allah's Creation, The Human Body
56. Childbirth and Reproduction
57. Islaamic Cooking Book
58. Children's Fables of Amir Abdullah
59. What is a Muslim?

60. What is a Prophet?
61. Intoxication is a sin
62. The Holy Gospel, The Revelation of Jesus, The Masiyh (Messiah) To The World (In Volumes)
63. Islaamic games for Muslim children, Book 1
64. Opening of the Seventh Seal, Secret Societies Unmasked
65. Science of Creation
66. The True Origin of Martial Arts
67. Will Send Elijah, Before The Coming of The Great and Dreadful Day of The Lord.
68. Christ Is The Answer
69. The Raatib (Unshakable) of Imaam Al Mahdi
70. Family Guide to Easy Arabic Phrases
71. Arabic Reader
72. Arabic, The First Language
73. Arabic Math Book One
74. Arabic Tape and Lesson One/Learn Your Language
75. Qur'aanic Tape and Lesson One
76. What and Where Is Hell?
77. Khutbah's (Sermons) of As Sayyid Al Imaam Isa Al Haadi Al Mahdi
78. What are Angels?
79. Animals of The Bible
80. How The Prophet Muhammad Read The Qur'aan
81. Learn How To Tell Time In Arabic
82. Santa or Satan: The Fallacy of Christmas (English/Spanish)
83. The True Story of Noah (Part 1 & 2)
84. Who, What & Where Is The Devil (Pt 1 & 2)
85. Ancient Egypt And The Pharaohs
86. Islaamic Beauty Aids And Customs
87. The Final Word
88. Muslim Funeral Rites
89. Series of Hadiyth
90. Prehistoric Man And Animals, Did They Exist?
91. The True Story of Abraham

92. Holy War (Jihaad)
93. Children's Book of Arabic (Ed. 1)
94. Slave Trade
95. He's A Disease
96. Ninety-Nine Plus Names of Allah
97. Seminars of As Sayyid Al Imaam Isa Al Haadi Al Mahdi
98. The Sex Life of A Muslim (Pt 2)
99. Who Was The Prophet Johan?
100. The Message Of The Messenger Is Right And Exact: The Book Of Laam (Pt 1)
101. The Message Of The Messenger Is Right And Exact: The Book Of Laam (Pt 2)
102. The Children's First Book In The Arabic Language (Book 1)
103. The True Story Of Cain And Abel
104. Halloween (English/Spanish)
105. The Fallacy of Easter
106. Islaam The True Faith, The Religion Of Humanity (Shaikh Da'wud)
107. Our Universe
108. Simplified Religious Book Of Arabic - Children's Edition (In Parts)
109. Who Was Noble Drew Ali?
110. The Holy Shroud: Fact or Fiction?
111. Jesus' Disciples: For Or Against Him?
112. English/Arabic, Arabic/English Vocabulary
113. How To Learn To Write Arabic
114. Teach Yourself Qur'aan (With Tape)
115. How To Read Qur'aan In Arabic
116. I Don't Claim To Be
117. Simplified Arabic Grammar
118. Contradictions Of The Disciples
119. The True Story Of Adam And Eve
120. The True Story Of Enoch (Idriys)
121. Racism In Islaam (Pt 1 & 2)
122. Read In Arabic For Beginners (In Parts)

123. Al Imaam Isa vs. The Computer
124. Beginners Arabic - Simplified Arabic Reading
125. The Pictures of The Arabic Alphabet Arabic Reading (Bk.1& 2)
126. Simple Steps To Teach Your Children Arabic Reading (Bk.1&2)
127. 127. Arabic Religious Classes (For Muslim Children)
128. As Sayyid Al Imaam Isa Al Haadi Al Mahdi Explains The Secret Meanings Of The Qur'aan To The A'immah Of Ansaaru Allah (In Parts)
129. The Arabic Penmanship Book
130. The Untold Story Of Jesus The Messiah (Pt 1 & 2)
131. The True Story of Yuwsuwf
132. Who Was The Comforter?
133. Ansaar's Guide Through Qur'aan For Better Living
134. Sacrifice: An Accord Of Islaam
135. Thus Said Al Imaam Muhammad Ahmad Al Mahdi
136. Examples And Conjugations Of Arabic Verbs
137. You Must Be Born Again (Shahadda) Pt 1&2
138. The Man Of Miracles In This Day And Time (Pt 1&2)
139. The Prophet Muhammad And Ali Were Nubian (Black)
140. Who Are The Nubian Islaamic Hebrews?
141. Gospel Of John Chapter 1
142. Gospel Of John Chapter 14
143. Gospel Of John Chapter 16
144. Should Muslims Observe The Sabbath?
145. You Are Adam's Descendants
146. Women Who Have Changed The Course Of History
147. Ahmad, Jesus' Khalifat (Successor)
148. Gospel Of Barnabas Book 1
149. Gospel Of Barnabas Book 2
150. Gospel Of Barnabas Book 3
151. Gospel Of Barnabas Book 4
152. The Book Of Laam, Fear No Longer For I Have Arrived
153. The Real Personality Of Jesus

154. Why So Many Kinds Of Muslims?
155. The Reading (30 Parts [Juz] Of The Qur'aan)
156. Qur'aanic Arabic Lessons For The Nubian Islaamic Hebrews (In Parts)
157. Where Is The Tabernacle Of The Most High (Pt1&2)
158. Allah Decides Who's Who In The Earth

Why didn't people Magazine or Christine Pelisek mention the amount of books that Dr. York had written at the time? Because it goes against the sensationalism that paints Dr. York as a monster. Here's a listing of books Dr. York wrote after 1986 A.D.

159. The savior
160. Women of the scriptures
161. Peaceful Sabbath
162. The truth of the scriptures
163. The true faces of the men of the scriptures
164. Circumcision
165. The faces of the people of the scriptures
166. Are there Orientals in the bible?
167. The making of the disciples
168. True story of the beginning
169. In the 60's
170. 666- mark of the beast
171. Are you still eating pork?
172. Seven heads, ten horns
173. Prophecy fulfilled
174. Muhammad was a Hebrew
175. If Jesus returns then what?
176. Nebuchadnezzar Era
177. Collage of truth
178. Nubic language/ Fallacy of Halloween (revised)
179. First language (revised)
180. Right knowledge (revised)
181. The lost tribe (revised)

182. Our true roots (revised)
183. Our bondage (revised)
184. The bible is his story
185. Right knowledge
186. Mythology (revised)
187. The bible is his-story
188. What is Nuwau-pu?
189. Breaking the spell
190. Garden of Eden (revised)
191. What is Nuwaupu? (revised)
192. Leviathan 666 (revised)
193. Let's set the record straight
194. Rizq and Illyuwn: fact or fiction?
195. Nuwaupu and Amunnubi Rooakhptah: the fact or fiction?
196. Are there black devils?
197. Does Dr. Malachi Z. York try to hide the fact that he was Imaam Issa?
198. Nibiru and the Anunnaqi: fact or fiction?
199. People of the Sun
200. Dr. York vs the computer
201. The great balls of fire cast at earth
202. The religion Islam unmasked
203. "GOD" "God" "god" what is the difference?
204. The body parts of god
205. What is god doing for you?
206. Let's talk about the end
207. God misinterpreted
208. Is god a wimp?
209. Where is the devil today?
210. Does the new testament contradict the koran?
211. Whose god is responsible?
212. Does god and the devil exist?
213. What is god's language?
214. Does god need religion?
215. Does religion breed ignorance?

216. Does god help his own?
217. Is Jesus the god of the koran?
218. Is Jesus the god of the koran? (revised)
219. Who is god?
220. God gave the sign to Jonah
221. Fake gods false Christ
222. Does god need love?
223. What is soul and spirit?
224. Sayings of Dr. Malachi Z. York
225. Is the Koran authentic?
226. Is Jesus god?
227. Sodom misinterpreted
228. Is there life after death?
229. What and where is Hell?
230. Humans were created from
231. Is god an extra-terrestrial?
232. Did god create the devil?
233. Is there a god pt.1?)
234. Is there a god (pt.2?)
235. Is there a god (pt.3?)
236. Conflict between the gods (revised)
237. Introduction of the Koran
238. Qur'aan Chapters 1-2
239. Qur'aan Chapters 3-4
240. Qur'aan Chapters 5-6
241. Qur'aan Chapters 7-8
242. Qur'aan Chapters 9-10
243. Introduction to Revelation
244. El Injiyl Chapters 1-11
245. El Injiyl Chapters 11-22
246. Introduction to Exodus
247. Exodus - The Torah-2 Chapters 1-12
248. Exodus - The Torah-2 Chapters 12-22
249. Exodus - The Torah-2 Chapters 22-31
250. Exodus - The Torah-2 Chapters 31-40

251. Introduction to Genesis
252. Genesis The Torah-1 Chapters 1-13
253. Genesis The Torah-1 Chapters 13-26
254. Genesis The Torah-1 Chapters 26-37
255. Genesis The Torah-1 Chapters 37-50
256. Introduction to Leviticus
257. Leviticus The Torah-3 Chapters 1-13
258. Leviticus The Torah-3 Chapters 13-27
259. Introduction to Numbers
260. Numbers The Torah-4 Chapters 1-9
261. Numbers The Torah-4 Chapters 9-19
262. Numbers The Torah-4 Chapters 19-29
263. Numbers The Torah-4 Chapters 29-36
264. Introduction to Deuteronomy
265. Deuteronomy The Torah-5 Chapters 1-10
266. Deuteronomy The Torah-5 Chapters 10-24
267. Deuteronomy The Torah-5 Chapters 24-34
268. Introduction to Ezra
269. Ezra Chapters 1-10
270. Debates with Christians (series Bk.1-10)
271. Debate with Muslims (series Bk.3)
272. Q & A, Debate and Discussion (series Bk.4)
273. Q & A, Debate and Discussion (series Bk.5)
274. Q & A, Debate and Discussion (series Bk.6)
275. Q & A, Debate and Discussion (series Bk.7)
276. Debates with Jehovah's witnesses (Bk. 1-8)
277. 360 Question to ask a Hebrew Israelite (Pt.1-4)
278. 360 Question to ask a Christian (Pt.1-4)
279. 360 Question to ask the Israeli church
280. 360 Question to ask Orthodox Sunni Muslims (Pt. 1-7)
281. The Holy Sabbath
282. Bane Mitzwah Ceremony
283. Circumcision Ceremony
284. The Birth Ceremony
285. Baptism Ceremony

286. Marriage Ceremony
287. Naming Ceremony
288. Man from Planet Rizq
289. Science of creation
290. Mission earth and the extraterrestrial involvement
291. Who lived before Adam and Eve story?
292. The mystery clouds, are they UFO'S?
293. Are there (UFO'S) extraterrestrials in our midst?
294. Shamballah and Aghaarta, cities within the earth
295. Melanin-ite children
296. Extraterrestrial and creation
297. Muslim's creed true or false?
298. Enoshites- Key of Life and the Covenant
299. Are There UFOs Extraterrestrials in Your Midst?
300. El's holy tablets (pt. 1,2,3 and 4)
301. El's holy torah
302. El's holy injiyl
303. E'ls holy tehilim (psalms)
304. E'ls holy Qur'aan (the noble koran)
305. Black book
306. Gold book
307. The Prophet
308. Scroll of Malachi
309. The book of the dead (coming forth by day)
310. Your potential (revised
311. The mind (revised)
312. The book of light
313. Sacred wisdom of Tehuti
314. The Degree of Moses-Ism
315. The Degree of Christ-Ism
316. The Degree of Muhammad-Ism
317. The little guide book for nuwaupians
318. The Holy tabernacle family guide book
319. Holy tabernacle's guide to better living
320. Nuwaubian taful (prayer)- revised

321. El maguraj- the pilgrimage (revised)
322. Nuwaupian calander
323. Grandma's words of wisdom
324. The teacher's guide to the nuwaupian language
325. Nuwaupic grammar
326. Nuwaupic at a glance
327. Nuwaupic simplified
328. Esoteric or exoteric
329. The egiptian deities in your mind
330. You and the ancient egiptian order
331. The sphinx and egiptian magic
332. The holographic brain
333. The eyes tunnel vision to the soul
334. Ancient egiptian wisdom
335. The wisdom of the egiptian mystic
336. Amun-Hotep son of hapi
337. Spoken words of ancient egiptians
338. Ancient egipt and the magic word of power
339. Egiptian thoughts
340. The sacred tones
341. The original egiptians were negroid
342. Magic word of ra
343. The egiptian book of Anubis
344. Its alignment time
345. Charms and amulets
346. The ancient egiptian sacred geometry
347. Link to the deities
348. The 9 principles in the human being
349. Bad habits
350. Communication with the deities
351. Pa ashutaat (the prayer)
352. Being an egiptian initiate
353. Ancient egiptian materialization rites
354. Egiptian secret on concentration
355. The breath

356. The egiptian healing temple ritual
357. The ancient egiptian martial arts
358. The ancient egiptian law and order
359. WU-NUPU the game of the ancient egiptian order
360. A.E.O constitution
361. The bes kept secrets are best kept sacred (mum's the word).
362. The decision
363. Psalms of Yaanuwn
364. E.A.
365. F.C.
366. M.M.
367. Hams seed
368. Paa gatut(revised)
369. Aset, asar, nebtat, wu satukh
370. Void and darkness
371. Enki as creator
372. Feeding the forces(revised)
373. The destroyer
374. Celtics(revised)
375. Paa Quadity(revised)
376. Wu-Nuwaupu(revised)
377. Zdihuti's vision(revised)
378. Nuwaupians ontologist of time
379. The procession change
380. Birth of religion
381. Emotional energy
382. Tones sounds DNA molecules vibrational frequencies
383. Who is god female or male?(revised)
384. The lost records of time
385. Image of the beast
386. 18+18+1=37 Genes of mitochondrial DNA
387. The gospel of Yaanuwn on the sacred feminine, the lotus of life.
388. Who you are not what you accept
389. Genetic kiss

390. The cycles
391. Existence how and why?
392. Is egiptian ontology or mythology?
393. Big foot
394. The supreme beings, melanin-ite beings
395. The proof
396. Neuroscience of Wunuwaup
397. The god of light and fire
398. Intelligent design, Divine design or plot of alien?
399. Sex, minds and slave
400. Natural ether energy
401. The guidance
402. Good and evil
403. Akasha records
404. You need me I don't I don't need you
405. Hell, on earth
406. The way
407. The monkey and the tree
408. Fact of facts
409. The last will be standing
410. What kind of god are you really worshiping
411. The warner
412. Woe nuwaupians
413. "A proclamation" "fruits"
414. What fools ye mortals be
415. Three types of love
416. Our sacred feminine
417. Your children
418. The accused
419. Diagnosis of the race
420. Paa antkuum
421. Ranankuum
422. Atlantis
423. The unclean issue
424. The nuwaupian man

425. The dimensional shift
426. The prism
427. Djedi wu zdahuti-mus
428. Paa paut, the all expanding
429. The planet earth is women
430. Creators, fashioners and makers
431. The ghost
432. The argument
433. The minds eyes
434. Paa banan-u
435. Goddess creators
436. The golden children
437. Conscious being
438. Power of the language
439. Black is evil, white is good
440. Black magic white magic
441. Sex force spirit force
442. Soul, soul, spirit, spirit
443. Thirty spirits
444. Sarab-u wu karab-u
445. Soulmates
446. The flood
447. Division
448. Kalal A'aaruf awuw tem A'aaruf
449. Rams as lambs
450. Relaxation
451. Fret, chafe, worry
452. Speaking of tongue
453. The age of the adamites past
454. Our tone wavelength "A"
455. The instigators
456. The formation
457. The emotion and the apostates
458. Wu-Nuwaup commandments on sexual violations
459. Concentration

460. I was there which is here Pt.1
461. I was there which is here Pt.2
462. Birth of earth and the matrix
463. Black dot, helix, and mind link mine linked
464. Your dimensional links, nabat, the sacred ash
465. No help from above, judgment upon the adamites
466. The Secret of the tones and the mafkhuzhat "elixir of life"
467. Factology of time
468. The bloodlust and religion
469. Ancient signs of speech
470. The cycles of life and death
471. The jewels of my divine eyes
472. The ultimate reality
473. Divide and conquer
474. Salvation
475. Those who lie and the who deceive Pt.1-2
476. The adamites law on killing and those who replace them
477. The tree of life
478. A nation of our own Pt.1-2
479. The spiritual you after the physical you dies
480. The truth
481. The physical ether
482. The designer genes
483. Many names
484. The twenty-four elders Pt.1-2
485. Trapped by way of religion
486. The Annunaqi and the Biblical and Quraanic race

Dr. York's works speak for themselves. It's obvious why People Magazine did not present SOME of Dr. York's life's work and that is because you would see Dr. York for who and what he really is, a Reformer and Master Teacher! Also bear in mind if People Magazine can leave out 486 books which consists of DECADES of Dr. York's life, then what else are they leaving out?

Tracy Bowen [pictured across] - **(Deputy Sheriff Putnam County)** - *"York's behavior was that of a typical Pedophile. It completely starts out with gaining their trust. I think in this case the first and foremost step in this process was that your parent is telling you that this is God and this is our Savior. So they believed they were suppose to do what ever they needed to do to please him (Dr. York)."*

Fact - There is no such thing as a "typical pedophile." During Dr. York's 2004 trial Kenneth Lanning (Government's witness, former FBI agent for 30 years) testified as an expert witness in the sexual victimization of children. Concerning sexual offenders against children or as Tracy Bowen said, "a typical pedophile"; this is what Kenneth Lanning revealed.

Kenneth Lanning - <u>One of the things that I discovered early on in studying **sex offenders against children** is what a **varied and diverse** population it was. There were **many different behavior patterns** involved and **they weren't all the same.**</u>
[January 7, 2004 A.D. Trial Testimony Case 5:02-CR-27-CAR]

Tracy Bowen made the statement "typical pedophile" for those who don't know that the fact is there is no such thing. By virtue of the fact that she's a Deputy Sheriff in a position of public trust, the public will trust her statements. As a Deputy Sheriff you have a responsibility and obligation to deal justly and fair and to avoid sensationalism.

Tracy Bowen - *"It completely starts out with gaining their trust."*

Fact - Dr. York has gained the trust of thousands of people throughout the years who have read his literature and heard him teach because his motto since 1970 A.D. until the very day of his arrest has been, **"DON'T BELIEVE ME, CHECK IT OUT."** Once people researched and investigated Dr. York and found his works to be FACTS; Yes, their trust was gained. Also, note the following:

Mr. Arora (Defense Attorney) - *"You could fit some of these characteristics and still be an innocent man; correct?"*
Kenneth Lanning - *"Yes; and that's why you have to look at the totality of facts and evidence and how you use this typology. This is not a typology to convict somebody. This is not a typology to say that because you have these traits, therefore, you must be guilty."*
   [January 7, 2004 A.D. Trial Testimony Case 5:02-CR-27-CAR]

Tracy Bowen - *"I think in this case the first and foremost step in this process was that your parent is telling you that this is God and this is our Savior."*

Fact - What makes this statement out of Tracy Bowen's mouth so ridiculous is the fact that 9 minutes into the very broadcast that came on where Tracy Bowen made the statement; There is a video clip of Dr. York teaching and he says to the listening audience and I quote, *"If he [Matthew 6:9 Our Father which art in Heaven] is my father and I am his son, and my father is what I am, and I am what my father is; When you see me you see my father, then when you see me, you see God.* **You are God incarnate and You, and You, and You, and You, and You, and You, and You."** This was actually in the broadcast. Tracy Bowen is depending on the public to just say, "Oh, she's a Deputy Sheriff; What she's saying must be true."

It's dangerous to have people in positions of public trust that don't have all their marbles. Dr. York is saying the very same thing that Jesus said in **John 10:33-34** to a group of Jews who accused Jesus of Blasphemy for being a man and calling himself a God. Jesus responded to them by saying "Is it not written in your law, I said, Ye are gods?" (**Refer to John 10:33-34**). Dr. York has repeatedly taught throughout the years and I quote **The Millennium Book pg. 446,** "<u>**When I say I'm god, I also say, That you, all of us are the children of God, (Psalm 82:6) not just me. I am no more god than you are.**</u>"

Tracy Bowen - *"your parent is telling you that this is God and this is our Savior."*

Fact - We already clarified the "god" issue above. The Government is well aware of a Savior coming (Refer to Introduction). Also, the FBI Memorandum (in part) dated March 4, 1968 A.D. objectives was to prevent the rise of a Black Messiah (Savior). Dr. York rightfully and unapologetically is our (Nuwaupians) Savior. You will not give Nuwaupians a guilt complex for calling Dr. Malachi Z. York "Our Savior." When Jean Vanier passed away at the age of 90, the New York Times had no problem calling him a Savior. (Refer to May 7, 2019 article in **New York Times** entitled **"Jean Vanier, Savior of People on the Margins, Dies at 90"**). Just because "People Magazine" says something, doesn't make it factual as has already been revealed. We are not waiting for any person regardless of race to give us their stamp of approval or permission to call The Master Teacher Dr. Malachi Z. York Our Savior.

Jess Cagle - *"York tells them that in the Sudan where he claims to trace his roots from, that it is absolutely normal for an Elder man in the family to teach young girls about sex."*

Fact - Niki (Nicole Lopez) is part of the culprit of propagating this falsehood. During her trial testimony in 2004 in the case of USA vs York she says the following while under Direct Examination by Ms. Thacker.

Ms. Thacker - *"During this time (age 13), Ms. Lopez, did anyone ever discuss sex with you?"*
Niki (Nicole Lopez) - *"There was Nathara...Nathara used to talk to me about sex stuff."*
Ms. Thacker - *"And Nathara, what did she tell you about sex?"*
Niki (Nicole Lopez) - *"I know with me, per se, she started telling me, you know, like in Sudan or different countries, you know, there was a person in the family who would teach you about sex."*

[January 7, 2004 A.D. Trial Testimony Case 5:02-CR-27-CAR]

Another part of the culprit responsible for propagating the falsehood that Jess Cagle repeated was Habiybah "Abigail" Washington. Like "Niki" (Nicole Lopez) she was also given immunity from prosecution in exchange for her testimony according to 2004 A.D. Trial Transcripts in the case of USA vs York and we quote:

Mr. Moultrie - *"Now, before I ask you any other questions, I want you to tell the jury if you entered into an agreement between you and the government that involved an immunity agreement."*
Habiybah Washington - *"Yes, I did."*
Mr. Moultrie - *"And what did you understand your agreement to be with the government concerning that immunity agreement?"*
Habiybah Washington - *"I understood it to mean that I was cooperating with the government and my testimony would not be used against me."*
Mr. Moultrie - *"And what did you understand your responsibility to be with respect to your testimony?"*
Habiybah Washington - *"To tell the truth."*

[January 12, 2004 A.D. Trial Testimony Case 5:02-CR-27-CAR]

Habiybah Washington and the important part she plays will be addressed also. I don't blame Jess Cagle for speaking misinformation because I overstand where he gets it from. Saying of Dr. York ~ "Don't look and blame, See and overstand."

Niki - *"When I was 13 years old one of the wives, she had a conversation with me and said York would be the person that would teach me about sex and she would help me and talk to me because these are things you want to know as a growing woman."*

Fact - "Niki" (Nicole Lopez) is making reference to a character by the name of "Nathara" that was mentioned above which will be repeated below:

Ms. Thacker - *"During this time (age 13), Ms. Lopez, did anyone ever discuss sex with you?"*
Niki (Nicole Lopez) - *"There was Nathara...Nathara used to talk to me about sex stuff."*
Ms. Thacker - *"And Nathara, what did she tell you about sex?"*

Niki (Nicole Lopez) - *"I know with me, per se, she started telling me, you know, like in Sudan or different countries, you know, there was a person in the family who would teach you about sex."*
    [January 7, 2004 A.D. Trial Testimony Case 5:02-CR-27-CAR]

Fact - There was no Nathara because "Niki" (Nicole Lopez) made her up. Nathara was not subpoenaed because she could not be found. No one knew where she was. There was no Photos of Nathara. Nathara was only known by "Niki" (Nicole Lopez) and Habiybah Washington who were the only 2 people given immunity agreements. How ironic. The Trial Transcripts below reveal that.

Mr. Arora (Defense Attorney) - *"Now we're gonna have some Sixth Amendment issues at this point too...but we're going into areas with people that, I mean, I can't possibly ever challenge; I have to take her [Nicole Lopez] word for it."*
    [January 7, 2004 A.D. Trial Testimony Case 5:02-CR-27-CAR]

Fact - The Sixth Amendment issue that Mr. Arora is speaking about is the right to confront your accusers. The testimony by "Niki" (Nicole Lopez) that was allegedly made by "Nathara" cannot be cross examined because "Nathara" can't be located. Trial transcripts below reveal that fact.

Mr. Davis (Defense Attorney) - *"Where is she (Nathara) now?"*
Niki (Nicole Lopez) - *"Nobody knows."*
    [January 7, 2004 A.D. Trial Testimony Case 5:02-CR-27-CAR]

Fact - Defense Attorney Adrian Patrick also addressed the "Nathara" myth in his Final Argument below:

Mr. Patrick - *"Now, another thing, the **"Nathara"** or **"Nathada"** person, if there's actually a Nathada or Nathara that was actually the one to introduce **Abigail Washington** and **Nicole Lopez** to sex, why didn't the government bring her in? They mentioned Rodeya. We know who Rodeya is. We subpoenaed Rodeya to come. If there was a Nathara, why wasn't she here? They presented no picture of her to you. Rodeya didn't know of a **Nathara**. Mildred Cosme, who has been a member of the organization since '81, never heard of a Nathara. **There's no Nathara**. They created that so they can create someone to make it appear that someone brought them there."*
    [January 22, 2004 A.D. Final Argument by Mr. Patrick on Behalf of the Defendant (Dr. York) Case 5:02-CR-27-CAR]

Narrator - *"At this time no one on the outside really has any clue about the sex crimes going on inside the cult, but Law Enforcement is starting to investigate other criminal activity that York is connected to in New York City."*

Fact - Nicole Lopez (Niki) was born April 19, 1975 A.D. *"At this time"* is approximately 1988 A.D or 1989 A.D. because "Niki" gives a reference point by saying "When I was 13 years old one of the wives, she had a conversation with me..." The Ansaarullah Community

"At this time" is 18 years of people coming in and leaving and *"no one on the outside really has any clue about the sex crimes"*??? These alleged "sex crimes" are pertaining to Dr. York, who's supposed to be this Monster Serial Pedophile and there is not even a clue that this is going on with all the people who left throughout those 18 plus years?

Narrator - *"inside the cult"*

Fact - The Ansaarullah Community was headquartered in Brooklyn, New York. It was the axis that the OTHER COMMUNITIES revolved around. Communities existed in other cities such as Chicago, Detroit, Philadelphia, Baltimore, Atlanta, Pittsburg, Trinidad W.I. and London, England etc. The impression that People Magazine would like to stamp in the minds of the public is that Dr. York and the Community where he lived was the ONLY Community isolated off in some remote area surrounded with barb wire fences like a Military Base or Prison. Falsehood will perish in time because the Truth has arrived. Saying of Dr. York - **"Just be patient."**

Let's see what New York had to say about Dr. York and his community *"At this time."* Refer to the **Newsday** article dated *June 1, 1989 A.D. by Jimmy Breslin* entitled "**Combatting Crime By Force - Of Will**" where he makes a comparison between 2 Neighborhoods, One is infested with drugs and crime and the other just 2 blocks and-a-half away is drug-free, crime-free and safe; I quote:
"But two blocks down you turn onto **Bushwick Avenue** *and suddenly here is a stretch of maybe 2 and-a-half blocks, and the side streets* **where no drug seller dares set foot**. *This part of Bushwick Avenue and Hart and Suydam Streets, is the home of the Muslim Order, The Nubian Islamic Hebrews. Men in long white robes wearing white skullcaps sit on chairs at the street corners or patrol the sidewalks. They are of good size and quite mannerly, but they are there. The old Bushwick Avenue homes are spectacular and the*

sidewalks are lined with carnations and rose bushes. Women covered from head to foot by long robes walk by and children in tan shirts peer through the fence of a playground alongside a school the group runs. In the "Original Tents of Kedar" a store that sells religious pamphlets and tapes - "Learn Arabic by Tape" - four young men in white robes sat and watched a rap group on Television. A fan cooled the immaculate room. "Ones with drugs don't come here because of the example we set" one of them said. "They know we don't play" Abdullah Muhammad said, "We have no trouble here." How long since the last time you had any trouble? "I can't even remember the last time. More than 10 years. I'll tell you that. We are here for 21 years now. We don't tolerate anything." We set a good example here" Muhammad said "We don't drink and smoke and use drugs. In other places you have people setting an example of using drugs and selling drugs." One of the others said, "You can leave your car outside with the radio in it. Here, old ladies won't get their purse snatched." Outside, the street was tranquil, the carnation and roses turning the air sweet. The men in white watched. The women walked by with their faces covered. Agree with how **they live or not they run the only sidewalks in the city of New York where there is no such things as drugs**. *The Muslims, and their style, might become quite popular in several other neighborhoods this summer."*

Narrator - *"but Law Enforcement is starting to investigate other criminal activity that York is connected to in New York City."*

Fact - If the serpent and his seed was able to get into God's garden, let us not be deceived into thinking that they were/are not able to get within the gates of the Ansaaru Allah Community or any Congregation for that matter. These seeds have cast a negative light on the community from then til now. In the **Philadelphia Community** there was a man by the name of Laven McNeil who went by Abdul Hamiyd. *"While in the Ansaaru Allah Community in Philadelphia, he and an ex-Ansaar staged a robbery in the Springfield Mall located outside of Chester, Pennsylvania...When*

Abdul Hamiyd was propagating the Ansaar doctrine in downtown Chester, a Springfield police officer approached him and placed him under arrest for the robbery..." (**Refer to The Ansaar Cult Rebuttal to the Slanderers pg. 530 by Dr. York 1989 A.D.**) This was criminal activity that didn't have anything to do with Dr. York. Also, in the Philadelphia Community there was a woman by the name of Khadiyjah who was the husband of Abdul Hakiym who would dress improperly in front of a 16 year old named Musa. Khadiyjah eventually succeeded in having sex with the 16 year old Musa and as a result was put out of the Philadelphia Community. (**Refer to The Ansaar Cult Rebuttal to the Slanderers pg. 527 by Dr. York 1989 A.D.**) Niki (Nicole Lopez) like Khadiyjah from the Philadelphia Community was also put out of the community for having sex with a "*15 or 16*" year old - Kuwsh Muhammad (Martinez) while she was "*23 or 24*". We see that **HISTORY REPEATS ITSELF!** Refer to the Trial Transcripts Direct Examination by Ms. Thacker:

Ms. Thacker - *"Did you ever have sexual activity with Kuwsh Martinez?"*
Niki (Nicole Lopez) - *"Yes. Twice."*
Ms. Thacker - *"Okay. How old were you when those two incidents occurred?"*
Niki (Nicole Lopez) - *"I may have been 23 or 24."*
Ms. Thacker - *"And how old would Kuwsh have been?"*
Niki (Nicole Lopez) - *"He was either 15 or 16."*
  [January 8, 2004 A.D. Trial Testimony Case 5:02-CR-27-CAR]

Jalaine Ward FBI Agent (Retired) [pictured on the next page] - *"He had been investigated for a variety of different crimes in Brooklyn and as a result of their investigations he decided to move out of the state and to Eatonton, Georgia."*

Fact - Dr. Malachi Z. York did not move down to Eatonton, Georgia from Upstate New York because he was being investigated for a variety of crimes. Dr. York had longed to move down South for 3 reasons. One, the weather in Upstate New York in the Catskill Mountains was so harsh during the winter that Dr. York wanted to move to a warmer tolerable climate. Two, Dr. York chose the land in Eatonton, Georgia because it was close to Rock Eagle Mound, a sacred Native American landmark which ties into his Native American Tribal name and heritage as Chief: Black Eagle which he was known as in Upstate New York where he lived on a Shushuni Nubian Tribal Reservation called "The New Foundation" before even moving down South. (**Refer to The Book Of The Five Percenters pg. 122 by Dr. York 1991 A.D.**) Three, because of assassination attempts on Dr. York's life. One such attempt was done by El Sayed Nosair who assassinated Rabbi Meir Kahane November 5, 1990 A.D. and was also linked with the bombing of the World Trade

Center in 1993 A.D. El Sayed Nosair visited the Community on April 22, 1990 A.D. planning to assassinate Dr. York, However, The Most High has a plan for Dr. York, And The Most High is the best of planners.

Sheriff Sills [pictured below] - *"The property was out in Putnam County in a very rural area, little over 400 acres. Much of it was bordered by the National Forest. Isolation was very much a factor. They were coming to Georgia and they were going to form their own Nation not subject to the laws of the United States."*

Fact - When Sheriff Sills says, "They were coming to Georgia and they were going to form their own Nation" What he has to remember is that The Yamassee Tribe of Native American Moors of which Dr. York is the Chief of, has roots in Georgia that predates the establishment of the "United States." The Yamassee war of 1715 shows that the Yamassee were fighting European Colonial powers 60+ years before The United States was born. Also to mention, the state of Georgia was the first state to forcibly remove Native Americans from their lands (**Refer to the Indian Removal Act of 1830 signed into law by Andrew Jackson, the 7th President**). The Yamassee are the descendants of the Olmecs who were the foundation of many Native American Tribes. The Olmecs were undoubtedly Nubian as the large Olmec Head Stones in Mesoamerica exhibit Negroid features of thick lips and wide noses. The Yamassee had their own history, culture, language and territory. That's the definition of a NATION. Dr. York and his community were not forming a Nation, They WERE and ARE a Nation. Dr. York gave Nubians back their history by teaching them the facts concerning Great Nubian Leaders of the Past, Present and Future; A culture rich in music, games, dress, doctrine to name a few; A very own language for Nuwaupians to communicate with one another in Nuwaupic; A territory that was taken once again by the State of Georgia who forcibly removed Nuwaupians; Yet the best is yet to come!

Sheriff Sills - *"not subject to the laws of the United States."*

Fact - The "United States" were colonies that seceded from Great Britain and declared their independence and then extinguished and conquered the Natives. The United States is not the Supreme Law or Power to whom all must be "subject" meaning beneath or inferior to. The United States was granted the right to exist and declare themselves independence. Now, Dr. York and Nuwaupians are here and have this same right and are not bound by the United States or anyone else to be who and what they are.

Jess Cagle - *"York's teachings take a very bizarre and unpredictable turn down in Georgia. What occurred in New York was just the tip of the Iceberg."*

Fact - *"unpredictable turn"* is just plain false. Dr. York predicted many times throughout the years prior to moving down to Georgia to his congregation of the changes that would take place and I quote the members:

Louise Eddington (Maryam Abdullah Muhammad) Brooklyn, New York
"I have been an Ansaar since May 30, 1972 A.D., Dr. Malachi Z. York told us years ago, that we wouldn't wear our veils anymore and

that we would have to change our clothes because it would become too dangerous. He told us way back then that we would be on our own land. So this metamorphosis that we are going through and have gone through in the past was expected."

Juanita Walker (Maryaam Abdullah Muhammad) Philadelphia, Pennsylvania

"I moved into the Ansaar Allah Community in 1979 A.D. ... He [Dr. York] told us that we would one day have to shed our Garbs. Some of the things that he is telling us is not by far, new or made up. He did warn us many times."

Bruce LaRoche (Abdul Wali Abdullah Muhammad) Brooklyn, New York

"I walked with Imaam Issa (Dr. York) from State Street, Islaamic Mission Of America under Sheikh Daoud. I was in Sheikh Daoud's Office when he declared Imaam Issa (Dr. York) his successor and even issued him a certificate...he (Dr. York) would say that Islaam is just one of the stages in our learning and that the veil and the lifestyle that we lived, We would outgrow. It would become too dangerous, for Pale Arabs would invade the Country with their devilishment. He would say that what he has to teach, We are not ready for it yet. But we must first go through these Schools of Religion before we would overstand Nuwaupu.

Evelyn Rivera (Aiyda Abdullah Muhammad) Santruce, Puerto Rico

"I moved into the Ansaaru Allah Community in 1977 A.D. Everything that Dr. Malachi Z. York has said is manifesting before our eyes. I can verify that he often told us that "One thing that is constant is change." And that's exactly what we've been through. And with every change came an era, a dress code, a flag, Major books and we've always had a language Classical Arabic - and Nubic. He would often tell us that there is so much that I (Dr. York) have to give to you However, you're not ready for it now; Therefore I have to

spoon-feed you this knowledge so that you will one day overstand. He told us one day that we would have to drop the Garb of the Righteous (The Jallabiyya and the Veils) because of what Islaam was going to become - Associated with Terrorism. And if we didn't we would be confused for or accused of being a part of that Terrorism." (**Refer to Does Dr. Malachi Z. York try to hide the fact that he was Imaam Issa? by Dr. York pg. 90-94, 1996 A.D.**)

As you can see Sensationalism boosts ratings and People Magazine did not do their due diligence.

Ruby Garnett - *"The doctrine started to change."*

Fact - Dr. York did not change the doctrine because Dr. York's doctrine is truth and facts. Dr. York only enhanced or increased the amount of truth and facts that he revealed.

Ruby Garnett - *"He said the Government would start targeting us if we stayed practicing Islam. He wanted us to blend in."*

Fact - First of all The Ansaaru Allah Community was like no other Community. Whenever Dr. York was asked if he was a Muslim, he would say "Insofar as the meaning of the word "Muslim" which is "One who is of peace." Dr. York made it very clear that he had absolutely nothing to do with East Arabs and has always said they were Hypocrites. Dr. York forewarned that Islam regardless of the sect was going to be associated with nothing but Terrorism, Bloodshed and Scandal. As the Leader of a Congregation Dr. York has a responsibility for the safety of his community. A good shepherd knows where to lead his flock.

Tracy Bowen (Deputy Sheriff Putnam County) - *"I can clearly remember the first time I had ever saw a Nuwaubian. I remember pulling up into the Grocery Store and seeing a mini-bus pull up; 15 to 20 people get off of the bus and they were dressed in Cowboy Garb,*

Hat, vest, boots, the big belt buckle. Completely not the way we dress here."

Fact - "Cowboy Garb" came from Native Americans. The "Cowboy" hat came from the "Indian Joe" hat. Europeans later blocked off the "Indian Joe" hat to what became known as the "Cowboy" hat seen in the cinemas and associated with "Westerns." "Cowboy" boots were worn by Native Americans which is why you see fringes on them. These fringes or tassels were part of dress code of the children of Israel (Numbers 15:38-40). Europeans came over to the Americas and picked up on the dress code of the Natives and adopted it. When Tracy Bowen says, "Completely not the way we dress here" she has to know that Nuwaupians are not trying to dress like YOU, look like YOU, think like YOU, act like YOU, talk like YOU, live like YOU and last but not least WORSHIP and IDOLIZE YOU. If she knew anything about Native American culture you would know that Nuwaupians were being who and what they are. Last but not least the term "Cowboy" is simply Cow and Boy. Europeans would refer to Nubians aka "blacks" derogatorily as boys and because of the harmonious interaction Nubians had with the cows that Europeans noticed, thus the slang name - "Cowboy."

Narrator - *"After a strange Western phase, York tries on several new identities and each one is more bizarre than the next."*

Fact - Due to the misinformation that has been programmed into the minds of the public through the medium called Television since the 20th Century many people get an image of a Clint Eastwood or John Wayne, Kurt Russell and Val Kilmer type character when they hear the term "Western. Prior to coming to Georgia; In Liberty, New York in the Catskill Mountains; Dr. York identified with his Native American Heritage by living on a Native American Reservation where he was known as Chief Black Eagle (pictured below).

Narrator - *"He claims to be Chief Black Thunderbird Eagle of the Yamassee Native American Moors of the Creek Nation."*

Fact - He simply is and Nuwaupians accept him as such.

Narrator - *"Then he calls himself Yaanuwn - an Extraterrestrial from another Planet."*

Fact - This is misleading because the Narrator says prior that Dr. York *"tries on several NEW IDENTITIES"* (Implying that Dr. York assumed this identity after moving to Georgia). Yaanuwn (Yanaan) is not a "New Identity." If you refer to **The Man Of Miracles In This Day And Time Part 1 Authored by Dr. York 1983 A.D pg. 23-24** Dr. York says and I quote: *"I feel sorry for the people who sit around and think I have the power to fabricate all of these things. If I did, I would probably spend my time writing movies as opposed to trying to raise the lost souls. I don't sit around and make these things up. These are distinct personalities of people, who have lived in the past or in other galaxies who incarnated into me and they relay* *their messages through me to you. This is what makes me different from most people. I am not saying that I am anything special as an individual. I am saying that these powers come through me and they are distinct people."...Each one of them represents a certain amount of information that must be conveyed in these last days and times. Some of them represent spirituality, some of them are healers, historians, great men and some of them accompanied great men. For instance:*

YAANAN - Is from another galaxy. He is a visitor"
Also, If you refer to the True Light Audio Cassette Tape entitled **Who and What are You?** that came out in the 1980s Dr. York taught and I quote: "*Yanaan is an extraterrestrial being who* **incarnates** *into the body of Imaam Isa (Dr. York) to pass on information to you.*" The word incarnate is from the Latin *in* which means *into* and *carn* which means *flesh*. Now let's break down the meaning of Extraterrestrial. *Extra* meaning *added* or *additional*. *Terra* is the Latin word for *earth* and *Astral* is from the Greek *astron* meaning a *star*. So we have something additional on the earth from a star constellation which has planets. Crazy? Sure, as crazy as when Jesus said in John 8:23 "*Ye are from beneath; I am from above; ye are of this world; I [Jesus] am not of this world.*" In this verse the word from which "*world*" is being translated from is the Greek word "*Kosmos*" which means "*Universe.*" A universe contains galaxies which contains stars which sustains planets which are other worlds. Jesus was born on earth yet he said he was from another world aka "Planet." Did an extra-terra-astral being "Light upon Jesus? Yes, in Matthew 3:16 it says in part "...*The heavens were opened unto him, and he saw the Spirit of God descending like a dove, and lighting upon him.*" The Greek word that "*heavens*" is being translated from is "*Ouranos*" which is "*Orion*" a star constellation. This is where the "*Spirit of God*" came from and "*lighted*" on Jesus. The word "*lighting*" is being translated from the Greek word "*erchomai*" which means "*accompany*" or "*enter.*" So in essence, the Spirit of God entered or incarnated into Jesus from another star constellation; That part of

Jesus that incarnated into his body was Extra-Terra-Astral. Now, you have a right to not accept Dr. York as Yaanuwn but you do not have a right to falsely accuse Dr. York because you do not accept him for who and what he is to Nuwaupians and others.

Niki (Nicole Lopez) - *"Through the changes York was making, we wanted to ask questions but we didn't want to seem like we're challenging his authority or his leadership.*

Fact - Had this statement been made about a man or woman who simply gives a lecture in front of an audience without ever opening up themselves for questions, it could be believable. But to say a man such as Dr. York who set up a forum where the public can ask questions not just on what Dr. York teaches, lectures and speaks about, but on ANYTHING the public has on their hearts and mind as well as the teachings, doctrines and beliefs of others and ANYTHING else; It's not by far a believable statement. This is the Information Age where everything is at the touch of your fingertips; Just go to YOUTUBE and search Dr. Malachi Z. York and you will see and especially hear countless classes given by Dr. York where he addresses questions of a challenging nature with no fear or hesitation; Many times baffling the questioner as to how Dr. York knows so many answers! As Dr. York would say "DON'T BELIEVE ME, CHECK IT OUT!"

Niki (Nicole Lopez) - *"He was really good at creating these stories, that it made sense in the moment."*

Fact - I'm glad Niki (Nicole Lopez) made this statement because now we are about to see how good Niki (Nicole Lopez) was at creating her false story about Dr. Malachi Z. York and the type of person she is. Niki (Nicole Lopez) wrote 2 Letters prior to her testimony during Dr. York's 2004 A.D. Trial which shows her promiscuous lifestyle and her deceitful nature.

LETTER NO. 1 FROM NIKI (NICOLE LOPEZ)

To Layla,
 How are you doing? I missed you very much. I miss your mom, she's cool, and of course you know **I definitely miss Kuwsh [minor who Niki was having sex with]. I wish I had the balls enough and left. Instead of being here pretending. I want to experience things, life, no worries, going places, smoking (and not cigarettes) getting drunk without guilt or stealing,** finding new experiences.. Talk about Christians waiting in vain 2,000 years for Jesus, as we sit on the land and wait in vain for Baba's [Dr. York] return, or a life. Both religion, both bullshit. The boys and girls have been giving their freedom to roam without anyone bothering them again from **Baba [Dr. York], Kayuse was trying to put all these rules on them. Anyway Shababa's party was funny. First Amanda & Beluwra [Krystal Hardin - alleged victim] got the "drinks" and not Zinfandel, the real shit - vodka and all.** We were trying to find a good spot...**Shaira [Barbara Noel - Niki's mom who tried to bribe Dr. York]** was sleep in the Attic. It was a Friday night. We had music + no lights. **Shelomoh[Abdul Salaam LaRoche - alleged victim]** was happy because he is always messing with Shababa. Shababa got wild, cursing, telling Isaam + **Shelomoh[Abdul Salaam LaRoche - alleged victim]** don't mess with her unless they're "ready." She cursed me out after she pulled me close and felt I had short hair. I tried to tell her I was growing it but she had got the fuck away from her

and she played in Amanda's hair. At one point **Shelomoh[Abdul Salaam LaRoche - alleged victim]** *was trying to grab me, tell me I was drunk (which I was) but I was pushing him back to Shababa,* **Beluwra [Krystal Hardin - alleged victim]** *got up and we were dancing to "Back that thing up" [Juvenile - Back that azz up] so you could imagine how that looked. I was scared to death when Isaam tried to join in because I never danced with the opposite sex before. He was trying to get me to loosen up but I froze. I kept going back for Vodka + Whiskey.* **Beluwra [Krystal Hardin - alleged victim]** *was cutting up falling on people, grabbing people. At one point I was laying down and Isaam had came over and* **Shelomoh[Abdul Salaam LaRoche - alleged victim]** *and* **Beluwra [Krystal Hardin - alleged victim]** *flew off the handle.* <u>*She started yelling at people and telling me [Niki] why don't I find* **Kuwsh [minor who Niki was having sex with]**</u>*, of course I cursed her right back out, telling her, I don't want your man. Then she tried to jump off the balcony. Isaam tried to stop her, but she asked him to join her! She was really tripping.* **Amanda [Amala Noel - alleged victim and Niki's sister]** *had an attitude because people kept getting on her bed (and because she was on her "rag") her bed is in front of the window. We kept trying to get Shababa to lay on the sleeping bag but she was not having it. Then they had to carry her to the bathroom. She made so much noise.* **Shaira [Barbara Noel - Niki's mom who tried to bribe Dr. York]** *came out and told them to turn off the music. She must have been half sleep not to notice* **Shelomoh** *in the chair.* **Shelomoh[Abdul Salaam LaRoche - alleged victim]** *kept trying to get blow jobs from* **Amanda [Amala Noel - alleged victim and Niki's sister]** *& them because he couldn't get it up. Isaam told him that can happen if he had too much to drink which he did because he tried to pin me to the bed 4 different times. Isaam had to tell him to get off. I barely had the energy to fight. Me and* **Amanda [Amala Noel - alleged victim and Niki's sister]** *had to sneak them through the front door at almost 4[am] in the morning... We all over slept the next morning.* **Amanda [Amala Noel - alleged victim and Niki's sister]** <u>*had 3 Zinfandels*</u> *in a locked bag that bitch Suhaila found while stealing stuff from*

Amanda [Amala Noel - alleged victim and Niki's sister]. *Of course she told* Abigail [witness given immunity], *but* Amanda [Amala Noel - alleged victim and Niki's sister] *said she found it cleaning up the Aset Fasha in the Pyramid but she was too "scared" to drink it. She is doing okay. She is not planning on writing Doc [Dr. York], even though he sent a message as to why other girls wrote but not her. She is who he is expecting the letter from. She still wants to leave. I wrote* **Kuwsh [minor who Niki was having sex with]** *and he didn't write me back. I had Solomon call him for me to say happy birthday. I also gave him a bunch of stamps. I don't know why he* **[Kuwsh - minor who Niki was having sex with]** *doesn't write me back. When he was here* **Beluwra [Krystal Hardin - alleged victim]** *would tell me a whole lot of shit, like he don't really like me like I like him or he calls me his bitch, or rips up my letters I give him without reading them. I was very hurt by that especially since I used to wait up until 5:30 in the morning waiting for him* **[Kuwsh - minor who Niki was having sex with]** *to come to Edfu when he was hanging with the girls in the sewing room.* **Shelomoh[Abdul Salaam LaRoche - alleged victim]** *said he heard about me and Isaam, he probably heard about the party, because there's nothing for him to "hear." Sometimes he is funny, because he will assume I am doing stuff with someone without asking, and if I was, like he didn't do stuff with the girls or fuck* Amanda [Amala Noel - alleged victim and Niki's sister] *after he fucked me, and I wasn't supposed to know. But none of that can change the way I have felt, feel and will probably always feel for him. I gave him my heart. Can't nobody else take. Going into the woods I got fired, Katherine got fired and put in Athens bookstore, she got a mate now. Sharika got kicked out for being sarcastic.* **Abigail [witness given immunity]** *asked was it my idea and what am I doing there. I said it was and we were bored and finished our work and was told we could go anywhere, so that's where we went. So now we found a bush to go through, so people don't see us. When I talked to* **Abigail [witness given immunity]** *I told her of things that bothered me like people teasing me, she said that was cruel (as if she wasn't one of the main ones) I am so tired of the games...I told my* mother 2 times I don't want to be here, she got mad and told me to rise above the negativity and see that there are forces pushing people out, I want to experience things...Kind of the opposite with me and Kuwsh. I opened up to him, but he couldn't do or say the same. I wish I would just wake up in his arms while he kisses my neck....One time me, **[Kuwsh - minor who Niki was having sex with]**, Isaam, and Sharika was talking about Love, they were trying to find out if I loved anyone....They kept trying to get the name **Kuwsh**...So when he **[Kuwsh - minor who Niki was having sex with]** was leaving I told David to tell him, he never found out the person. He **[Kuwsh - minor who Niki was having sex with]** told David, he is not stupid, he knows who it is and he loves me too! I could have died. I was smiling for a week. Nobody has ever told me that. Please if you see him tell him **Kuwsh - minor who Niki was having sex with]** to write me. I miss him and hopefully when I get the balls up I'll be with him **[Kuwsh - minor who Niki was having sex with]**"

    END OF 1ST LETTER

Letter No. 2 from Niki (Nicole Lopez)

"So we go to Namah's house. I was hoping they forgot. Then Dean slapped Namah's ass. She was like "oh shit that hurts." I was like I told you he got some heavy hands. Then Eli and Ish was hitting Namah's ass. I was laughing then they came to me. I was like "no." They was holding me down and slapped my ass, it hurted so bad. Then Eli took Namah in her room and was on her hitting her slapping her. I was laughing then I ran to help Namah, then Desa turned off the light, grabbed me and was hitting me. I was screaming, laughing, it was funny.

Holding my hand and arms. I couldn't move, then Eli was like "oh shit." Dean looked at this, he was playing with Namah's breast. Dean started laughing. Eli was getting hype, then Ish turned off the light and was messing with Namah. I was fighting Dean then Eli came and was feeling my nipples, squeezing it so hard. I was like "get off my breast" (calm down I had a shirt on) Then Eli was like "Oh Shit, They getting hard", then he put his mouth on my shirt. I was like get the fuck off of me, he totally disrespected me. Then Dean put his mouth on it and flipped me over. He was holding my arms so I couldn't move. Then my breast was all in his face. Then Ish came and slapped my ass. I was screaming then I was fighting Dean trying to get him off me. When all of a sudden he grabbed me in the bathroom and locked the door. I was like, let me out. We was just fighting then he got my arms, picked me up. I just know he was feeling on my ass, biting my cheeks, feeling my tits...Then he was picking me up off the floor. He put me on top of him. I could definitely feel his dick. It was so hard. Then Ish unlocked the door with a hanger. God-damn that bathroom was too foggy. It looked like we took a hot shower and I left the bathroom steamy. **I ["Niki" Nicole Lopez] was enjoying myself.** *I ran in the bathroom again and locked myself when all of a sudden I hear Namah, screaming. They pulled off her bra and all 3 of them is sucking her breast. I was so mad for her that shit is foul.* **But man Dean is rough, that's what I like.** *I told Dean he couldn't handle me, he was like "Yes I could" then he grabbed me and picked me up. I was like "Dean put me down."*

END OF 2ND LETTER
[Case 5:02-CR-00027-CAR Document 417 Filed 04/02/09]

Now, nowhere in **Niki's (Nicole Lopez)** letter is there a mention of Dr. York engaging in any sexual conduct with her, any minors, and alleged victims. There is no mention of any wrong doing on Dr. York's part. There is no mention of Dr. York drinking alcohol with anybody, smoking marijuana or cigarettes etc., soliciting anyone for sex or anything that Niki (Nicole Lopez) alleges Dr. York did. However, what is revealed is the promiscuous lifestyle of these alleged victims and how they were all enjoying themselves while drinking and engaging in sexual activity. "Niki" Nicole Lopez has the audacity to say that Dr. York was good at creating these stories; Yet we see how it was easy for her to create these stories because she actually committed these acts she claims Dr. York did and just colored and painted Dr. York in the picture. This was not hard for her to do because she was known for her "Fantastic Layout And Artwork" **[Refer to the "Gratitude" section of the Holy Tablets which was released in 1996 A.D. below which shows Nicole Renee Lopez]**

"Niki" Nicole Lopez came into the community as a clever child as her testimony reveals and I quote:

"Niki" (Nicole Lopez) - *"...when I was in schools before I came in the Mosque, I was always in like gifted classes or higher learning classes... And when I was supposed to go to school, I got chosen to go to the Art Institute."*

[January 8, 2004 A.D. Trial Testimony Case 5:02-CR-27-CAR]

Gratitude

First And Foremost All Gratitude Is Given To The Most High For My Very Existence. Next I'd Like To Thank

Dr. Haroline Mary Herbert
For All Her Labors In Getting This Work Out.

Dr. Sakinah Aneesah Parham
For Her Financial Help In Getting This Work Out

Dr. Habiyba Washington
Dr. Stacey Charlain Parker
Dr. Shandra Denean Stubbs
Dr. Istiyr Cole
Dr. Ebony Hill
Dr. Hajar Abd-Allah Muhammad
Dr. Carla Thomas
For All Their Secretarial Skills

Nichole Renee Lopez
Khadiyjah Merrit
Lisa Tarter
Jori Jeffery
Joyce Hayee
Evelyn Riviera
Atiyah Tatiyana Thomas
For Their Fantastic Layout And Artwork

And All The Proof Readers And Critics
I Thank You All

"You have to look at who is feeding you and not just what they feed you" ~ Saying of Dr. Malachi Z. York

Tracy Bowen (Deputy Sheriff Putnam County) - *"Once they started building statues and the pyramids and were expanding. It did start to build concern within the Community..."*

Fact - There was a REAL ESTATE PYRAMID in Eatonton, Georgia that was in Eatonton, Georgia BEFORE Dr. York and Nuwaupians built THEIR PYRAMIDS in Eatonton, Georgia on their land located on 404 Shady Dale Rd which were practically identical to the REAL ESTATE PYRAMID located on 994 Greensboro Road, Eatonton, GA 31024-5801 pictured below.

And here is one of the Pyramids that Dr. York and Nuwaupians had on their land:

Do you notice the similarity? Of course, so did Stevie Wonder. Now, Tracy Bowen said that once Dr. York and Nuwaupians "*started building* **statues** *and the* **pyramids** *and were expanding. It did start to build concern within the Community*" Notice that the "<u>**concern**</u>" is not clarified or explained. Let's see if we can find what the "concern" might be. If you refer to the article entitled **Space Invaders by Sylvester Monroe in Time Magazine dated July 12, 1999 A.D.** it says and I quote: *"They're the nicest people" says a young white waitress at Rusty's, a small diner in downtown Eatonton. "But* <u>**I'm afraid they [Nuwaupians] are trying to take over the town.**</u>*"* If you refer to the article entitled **Accusation of Racism from The Macon Telegraph dated August 8, 1999 A.D. by Hilary Hilliard and Rob Peecher** it says and I quote: "<u>**If they [Nuwaupians] do takeover" Poole [One of 4 voting members of Putnam Commission] said "a lot of people will move out.**</u>"

So pyramids are not a concern. Statues are not a concern because Stone Mountain Georgia - a tourist attraction with monumental carvings of confederate soldiers is in a place that served for the rebirth of the K.K.K. in 1915 A.D. It's not so much a Pyramid or statue that is the concern but rather the image that the artist is drawing on the Pyramid or the image that the statue is in that's the "Concern". When you see a statue such as Isis or Aset pictured below that was on the Land in the Nuwaupian Community of Eatonton, Georgia; Those who have no problem and praise the origin as well as the men of Stone Mountain may have a "Concern" about this statue of Isis or Aset.

This is very important for the minds of young Nubian women to see an image of a Goddess that looks like them. When you walk up to this statue you have to look UP to it and then when young Nubian girls look in the mirror they no longer have to look DOWN on themselves. But if you want Nubian children to look in the mirror and see YOU; We can see how those statues could be a "CONCERN." Here's another statue that was on the Land in The Nuwaupian Community.

"If there is any image to be made of the Messiah Jesus in this day and time it should be based on the scriptures - Revelation 1:14-15 ~ Dr. Malachi Z. York

Tracy Bowen - *"I recall receiving phone calls from people up North. They would say my son or daughters joined this Cult down there and every time I call down there they won't let me talk to him or her. There's armed guards at the gate with guns and they won't allow me access."*

Fact - Well, let's deal with a son who not only was a part of this Community and who grew up in it, wanted to leave but also called his father to come and get him to see if he was stopped by these armed guards at the gate who don't allow access. Refer to the testimony of Abdus Salaam "Shelomoh" LaRoche's - alleged victim Cross Examination By Adrian Patrick - Defense Attorney during Dr. York's 2004 Trial below:

Adrian Patrick - *"Now you stated that before you left, you went to the defendant [Dr. York] and asked could you leave; correct?"*
Salaam LaRoche - *"Yeah. Because of my Mom, I mean. I mean, I would have just left with my father, but my Mom was like, you know, "Make sure you tell York because York was like a father to you," this and that, you know."*
Adrian Patrick - <u>*"You had already called your father?"*</u>
Salaam LaRoche - *"Uh-huh (affirmative)"*
Adrian Patrick - *"And he said he was going to come get you?"*
Salaam LaRoche - *"Uh-huh (affirmative)"*
Adrian Patrick - *"So that wasn't a problem for you to just leave with your father; correct?"*
Salaam LaRoche - *"I mean, when I was younger it was, but as soon as I turned 16, I told my mother I wanted to leave...And she was, you know, upset. But, you know, I just left because I didn't want to be there no more."*
Adrian Patrick - *"But I'm saying none of the guards tried to stop you when your father came to get you, did they?*
Salaam LaRoche - *"<u>They tried to talk me into staying</u>; but, you know, that was about it -- <u>I still left</u>"*
Adrian Patrick - *"<u>Outside of just talking to you, I'm saying they didn't try to hold you by gunpoint, did they?</u>"*
Salaam LaRoche - *"No."*
Adrian Patrick - *"So you say you spoke with the defendant that you were leaving. He didn't say anything like, "Don't tell the police" or anything like that when you left, did he?"*
Salaam LaRoche - *"No, I don't think so. But I just remember at one point where he said, you know, <u>"Stay out of trouble."</u>*
Adrian Patrick - *"He just told you to stay out of trouble?"*

Salaam LaRoche - *"Yeah."*
Adrian Patrick - *"So basically, you could leave whenever you got ready to, once you turned 16; correct?*
Salaam LaRoche - *"No."*
Adrian Patrick - *"Huh?"*
Salaam LaRoche - *"Because you know what I'm saying? Because I was a minor, you know, and my Mom was my legal guardian -- and she was on the land, so, you know, I had no choice but to be on the land. And then my father got kicked off, and they said that he was a bum and that he was on the train. So if I got -- and, plus, I didn't know my family that I had out there --"*
Adrian Patrick - *"So did you call your father on the phone and say "Come get me" or --*
Salaam LaRoche - *"Uh-huh (affirmative)"*
Adrian Patrick - *"So nobody restricted you from using the phone to call your father; correct?"*
Salaam LaRoche - *"No. No. But there was a certain time that you couldn't use the phone though."*
Adrian Patrick - *"I mean, there was certain periods of time you could use the phone."*
Salaam LaRoche - *"Uh-huh (affirmative)"*
Adrian Patrick - *"And your Father came on the land --"*
Salaam LaRoche - *"Uh-huh (affirmative)"*
Adrian Patrick - *" -- got your clothes and you left; correct?"*
Salaam LaRoche - *"Yeah. And, you know, he told me*
Adrian Patrick - *"Hold on. Who are you saying, "He" told you?*
Salaam LaRoche - *"And he asked -- my father asked me, "Did you tell York you was leaving?" And I told him "Yeah" And I guess my father would have never probably picked me up if, you know, I guess, if York didn't approve of it or what not."*
Adrian Patrick - *"But, nevertheless, there was not any problem whatsoever for you to leave, was there?"*
Salaam LaRoche - *"No -- I mean, if it was a problem about me leaving, I still would've left anyway, but I would've snuck off or whatever.*

Adrian Patrick - *"But you didn't have to sneak off or anything? Your father came on the land, picked you up, and you left; correct?"*
Salaam LaRoche - *"Yeah."*
Adrian Patrick - *"And the person you asked whether or not you could leave was your mother; correct? When you were thinking about who to ask whether or not to leave, it was not the defendant; it was your mother; correct?"*
Salaam LaRoche - *"At first, I was thinking about just leaving and not telling my mother."*
Adrian Patrick - *"No, this is what I'm asking you; When you were deciding to leave, the first person you went to was your mother, not the defendant; correct?"*
Salaam LaRoche - *"Uh-huh (affirmative)"*
Adrian Patrick - *"So when you were thinking about leaving, you thought about asking permission from your mother; correct?"*
Salaam LaRoche - *"Uh-huh (affirmative)"*

[January 12, 2004 A.D. Trial Testimony Case 5:02-CR-27-CAR]

Fact - Salaam LaRoche called his father on the phone to come get him. **The guards talked to Salaam LaRoche** about staying but he still left with his Father who wasn't denied access onto the Land nor restricted from taking Salaam LaRoche off the Land **and neither one of them were held at gun point** during the process. On top of that Abdus Salaam did not ask Dr. York for permission to leave, he asked his mother. Furthermore for the record Abdus Salaam LaRoche "Shelomoh Eddington" wrote and I quote:

"I affirm that the reason I testified falsely against Malachi York and other aforementioned is because I was told that I had to go along with the stories as everyone else did. FBI Jalaine Ward told me and I quote, "Other people already came forth and we already know what happened and it's best that you do the same."

[Case 5:02-CR-00027-CAR Document 417 Filed 04/02/09]

········ Biographical Rebuttal To People Magazine ········

BTW [By the way] Salaam LaRoche according to The **ATHENS BANNER-HERALD article posted September 20, 2018 A.D.** was a murder suspect in the death of Pamela Crisler who was found stabbed to death August 21, 2002 A.D.

OnlineAthens
ATHENS BANNER-HERALD

Man pleads not guilty in 16-year-old alleged Athens murder

By Joe Johnson
Posted Sep 20, 2018 at 2:00 PM

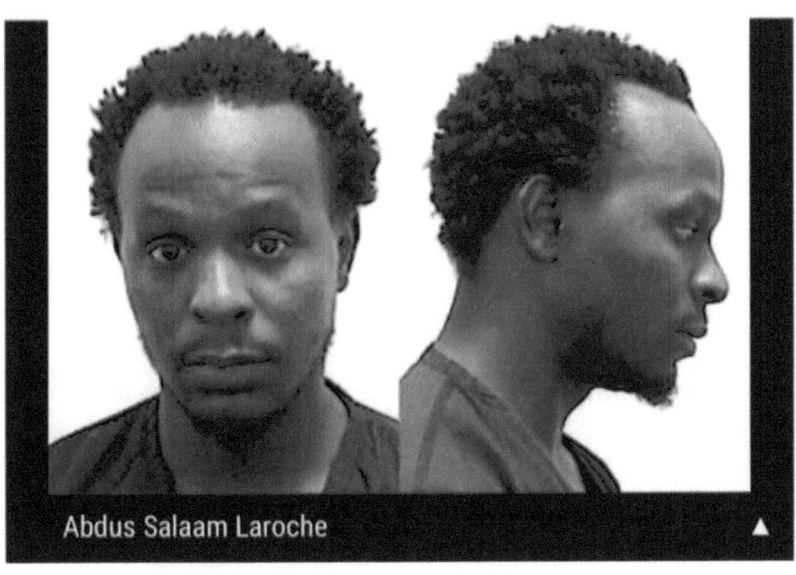

Abdus Salaam Laroche

A man this week pleaded not guilty to charges he fatally stabbed a woman in her westside apartment 16 years ago.

Abdus Salaam Laroche, 34, of Decatur was arrested May 8 for the 2002 alleged murder of 49-year-old Pamela Crisler in the mental health and substance abuse counselor's home at College Place Apartments. The complex off West Broad Street is now called University Oaks.

A grand jury in July indicted Laroche for malice murder, two counts of felony murder, first-degree burglary and aggravated assault, according to Clarke

County Superior Court records. He pleaded not guilty to all charges at his Monday arraignment.

Crisler's homicide case had grown cold until late last year when Laroche supplied a DNA sample when convicted of a felony in the Atlanta area, according to Athens-Clarke County police.

That sample was entered into the Combined DNA Index System, a national DNA database, and last November police in Athens were notified that Laroche's DNA matched genetic evidence found at the Crisler murder scene.

Laroche was arrested on May 8 following an investigation by police with the assistance of the DeKalb County Probation Office, the Georgia Bureau of Investigation and the FBI.

Notice how <u>Abdus Salaam LaRoche was arrested on May 8, 2018 and Dr. Malachi Z. York was arrested on May 8, 2002.</u> The Most High has all of their numbers and those that falsely accused Dr. Malachi Z. York will have their day in the light.

Woman being interviewed - *"To me it seems like they're trying to take over"*

Fact - Remember these 2 <u>articles 1.</u> **<u>Space Invaders by Sylvester Monroe in Time Magazine dated July 12, 1999 A.D</u>** it says and

I quote: *"They're the nicest people"* says a young white waitress at Rusty's, a small diner in downtown Eatonton. "But I'm afraid they [Nuwaupians] are **TRYING TO TAKE OVER** the town." And 2. **Accusation of Racism from The Macon Telegraph dated August 8, 1999 A.D. by Hilary Hilliard and Rob Peecher** it says and I quote: *"If they [Nuwaupians] DO TAKEOVER"* Poole *[One of 4 voting members of Putnam Commission] said "a lot of people will move out."* This is the 3rd time that concern of a TAKEOVER has been mentioned. One time is an incident, Two times is a co-incident and Three times is a reality. Dr. Malachi Z. York wasn't interested in Taking Over and I quote: **"When they saw us coming in Putnam County, this little old town, They said they're (Nuwaupians) gonna takeover. We wasn't interested in taking over. We came over here to be left alone."** (Refer to class entitled Do Women Have Souls According To The Bible? by Dr. Malachi Z. York)

Niki - *"We had security guards to guard people from not coming on to the Property, but we were not behind a gate with a lock-and-key."*

Fact - True. Many of us visited Tama-Re and can bear witness.

Niki - *"We were built up mentally believing that we couldn't leave, we shouldn't leave, we're sacrificing for the greater good, we're sacrificing for the future."*

Fact - Dr. Malachi Z. York has said many times that his job is to present the facts and the rest is up to you. Dr. York is not a Warden of a Prison, He's a Teacher and a Master at it. He doesn't force students to stay or come to class. If you refer to the video entitled **Part 6 of Dr. Malachi Z. York in 1992** which was recorded in Upstate New York Dr. York says and I quote **"A lot of people didn't stay on the boat with me like Columbus, I was like 'land is ahead,' they was like 'I don't see no land', 'this is getting ridiculous', 'I can't live like this', I'm leaving.' I was like "OK."** The Master Teacher Dr. Malachi Z. York taught and I quote: **"Anyone who**

wants to go, let them go...You don't want the Grace of God, You don't want to be a part of the Church...let them go their way. If it's meant like the prodigal son, they'll come home." (Refer to the class entitled Is The Root Of The Devil In Our Children by Dr. Malachi Z. York)

Furthermore Dr. York said on the class entitled (**Do Women Have Souls According To The Bible? by Dr. Malachi Z. York**) and I quote: "People leave me as they're leaving the Church they write me a letter "I'm not really leaving because of this, you know I really love the doctrine etc..." They will talk to you first, have a dialogue but they already planned to do what they want. That's why I don't bother talking to people anymore...I already know by this scripture (Genesis 4:6-9) that they already got their mind made up, that Cain was going to kill Abel anyway because that's what he wanted to do because he was jealous and he was mad and angry because things didn't go his way."

Niki (Nicole Lopez) was angry and bitter when she left the "Garden." Remember in **LETTER NO. 1 FROM NIKI (NICOLE LOPEZ)** she admits that she wanted to leave and was PRETENDING and I quote:

"I wish I had the balls enough and left. Instead of being here pretending. I want to experience things, life, no worries, going places, smoking (and not cigarettes) getting drunk without guilt or stealing.." So the things Niki wanted to experience must have NOT been what was advocated or tolerated within the community. Niki (Nicole Lopez) has been pretending to have been a victim when she is indeed the perpetrator and false accuser. Remember, Salaam LaRoche called his father on the phone to come get him. The guards talked to Salaam LaRoche about staying but he still left with his Father who wasn't denied access onto the Land nor restricted from taking Salaam LaRoche off the Land and neither one of them were held at gun point during the process. Dr. Malachi Z. York did not exercise this concocted control that Niki and these alleged victims fabricated.

The following testimony is from the **May 14, 2002 Hearing: (in part) Direct Examination by Defense Attorney Ed Garland of Leon Stewart Adams - Police Officer for the city of Macon, Georgia.**

Ed Garland: *Who inspired you to become a police officer?*
Leon Adams: *Dr. York*
Ed Garland: *There has been testimony here that Dr. York exercises a control on every movement and thought of people who are in that community and who share in the amenities there, Is that true?*
Leon Adams: *That has got to be the most ridiculous thing I've ever heard.*
Ed Garland: *Why do you say that's ridiculous?*
Leon Adams: *Dr. York encourages anyone that he has ever come in contact with to think for themselves.*

<u>IF</u> Dr. Malachi Z. York was committing all these covert, behind closed doors, illegal, heinous acts; Then that means that Dr. York had enough sense and intelligence to stay under the radar to not bring attention on his alleged illegal criminal acts; correct? So why would Dr. York allow the ones he was allegedly violating to leave the Community and have access to the outside world especially Law Enforcement to where all of Dr. York's SUPPOSED despicable acts could be brought to justice?! Wouldn't it make sense for a CULT LEADER to say, "You will not leave" or better yet plot to have these people "ELIMINATED?!" How is it that these alleged victims conveniently managed to leave this MONSTER?! The answer is simple, They lied on Dr. Malachi Z. York!!!

The "security guards" were the Nuwaupian Security force which was a necessity because on different occasions in the past the town's authorities have shown that they were no help. Nuwaupians have had hate mongers passing by the community flashing lights, shooting and shouting obscenities. When reported to the authorities there was no response. So the need for Nuwaupians own security force came about. The security force was registered under Max International Inc. The public is only being told one side of the story.

Ruby - *"One Morning I was cleaning up and I heard the door fly open and I saw one of my co-wives' daughters, she was crying and she was hysterical. She was screaming in Arabic that "Baba's #$%!& was in my mouth, Baba's #$%!& was in my mouth. She was only 5!!! I have never to this day seen anybody be that hysterical. She was hyper-ventilating. She couldn't catch her breath and she was crying. I held her and I calmed her down, it was heart breaking and I wanted to protect her* **BUT I COULDN'T**. *I thought about if he's doing that with her who else is he doing that with?* **This didn't make any sense to me**. *Everything I had believed was a lie..."*

Fact - This alleged **5 year old** girl manages to become **8 yrs old** in Ruby Garnette's book entitled **Soul Sacrifice: One Story of Many pg. 3** where she says and I quote: *"I was hearing this little 8yr. old girl scream out that the equivalent to what was her step-father had just had his penis in her mouth."* Ruby said *"I wanted to protect her [5 or 8yr. old girl] but I couldn't."* Ruby wasn't threatened or physically restricted from doing something. Now according to Ruby Garnette's book entitled **Soul Sacrifice: One Story of Many** she says on the foreword page ix and I quote: *"Someone who makes the choice to violate a child, or* **ALLOWS** *someone to violate a child is akin to being a* **devil**.*"* So by her own words this would render Ruby Garnette a devil because she allegedly ALLOWED a 5 or 8yr. old child to be violated by Dr. York. This alleged incident did not occur and Ruby Garnette is not a devil because of allowing this alleged incident; she is a devil because she is falsely accusing Dr. York of committing these acts. The word *devil* is from Greek *diabolos* and means *accuser, slanderer*.

Fact - Remember the **"Nathara"** character that was made up by Abigail Washington and Niki (Nicole Lopez) that supposedly introduced them to sex, who could not be verified? Guess who else used this character that couldn't be verified nor substantiated to write their book? Ruby Garnette. In **Soul Sacrifice: One Story of Many** pg. 144 she writes and I quote: *"I also noticed that when the* *girls came to visit, they were chaperoned by a sister named* **Nathara** *who was from Trinidad.* **Nathara** *was petite in stature; I'd say about 4'9" maybe 5', with light brown skin, and a face that was scattered with raised moles.* **Nathara** *was one of his [Dr. York] wives also...She was very hyper and sexually deviant, (I thought.)"* Quick recap to refresh your memory on this **"Nathara"** character below:

Ms. Thacker - *"During this time (age 13), Ms. Lopez, did anyone ever discuss sex with you?"*
Niki (Nicole Lopez) - *"There was <u>Nathara...Nathara</u> used to talk to me about sex stuff."*
Ms. Thacker - *"And <u>Nathara</u>, what did she tell you about sex?"*
Niki (Nicole Lopez) - *"I know with me, per se, she started telling me, you know, like in* **Sudan** *or different countries, you know, there was a person in the family who would teach you about sex."*
[January 7, 2004 A.D. Trial Testimony Case 5:02-CR-27-CAR]

Fact - There was no Nathara because "Niki" (Nicole Lopez) made her up. Nathara was not subpoenaed because she could not be found. No one knew where she was. There was no Photos of Nathara. Nathara was only known by "Niki" (Nicole Lopez) and Habiybah Washington who were the only 2 people given immunity agreements. How ironic. The Trial Transcripts below reveal that.

Mr. Arora (Defense Attorney) - *"Now we're gonna have some Sixth Amendment issues at this point too...but we're going into areas with people that, I mean. I can't possibly ever challenge; I have to take her [Nicole Lopez] word for it."*
[January 7, 2004 A.D. Trial Testimony Case 5:02-CR-27-CAR]

Fact - The Sixth Amendment issue that Mr. Arora is speaking about is the right to confront your accusers. The testimony by "Niki" (Nicole Lopez) that was allegedly made by "Nathara" cannot be cross examined because "Nathara" can't be located. Trial transcripts below reveal that fact.

Mr. Davis (Defense Attorney) - "**Where is she (Nathara) now?**"
Niki (Nicole Lopez) - "Nobody knows."

[January 7, 2004 A.d. Trial Testimony Case 5:02-Cr-27-Car]

Fact - Defense Attorney Adrian Patrick also addressed the "Nathara" myth in his Final Argument below:

Mr. Patrick - *"Now, another thing, the "**Nathara**" or "**Nathada**" person, if there's actually a Nathada or Nathara that was actually the one to introduce* **Abigail Washington** *and* **Nicole Lopez** *to sex, why didn't the government bring her in? They mentioned Rodeya. We know who Rodeya is. We subpoenaed Rodeya to come. If there was a Nathara, why wasn't she here? They presented no picture of her to you. Rodeya didn't know of a* **Nathara***. Mildred Cosme, who has been a member of the organization since '81, never heard of a Nathara.* **There's no Nathara.** *They created that so they can create someone to make it appear that someone brought them there."*

[January 22, 2004 A.D. Final Argument by Mr. Patrick on Behalf of the Defendant (Dr. York) Case 5:02-CR-27-CAR]

Jess Cagle - *"York does not physically stop his followers from leaving but he does brain-wash them into believing that they cannot survive on the outside without him.*

Fact - Because there is no history of Dr. York ever restraining someone from leaving the Community Jess Cagle has to say *"York does not physically stop his followers from leaving"* implying that Dr. York "mentally" restrains followers like **Shiloh** from **General Hospital**. If you refer to the class entitled **THE NEW COVENANT** *Dr. Malachi Z. York says and I quote:* "**I had many people who followed me years ago. Now they're out there following all kind of stupidity and fools but they'll never forget the truth I teach them.**" Dr. York is well aware of people who were once followers that left and joined other "communities" and are surviving "outside" without him. If you refer to the class entitled **WHY WE USED**

ISLAM Dr. Malachi Z. York says and I quote: "**All throughout the years I looked at that Congregation in Brooklyn, I'd give a khutbah [sermon] on Friday and I'd say y'all are faithful but y'all are not true. You will not last, very few of you. I said Many are called and few are chosen. Most of y'all will be out in the streets slandering me and doing everything the disciples of Jesus did.**" Furthermore to confirm that Dr. York was and is aware that "followers" would leave and be able to survive without him Dr. York wrote in **The Sons Of Canaan authored by Dr. York, 1987 A.D. pg. 2** and I quote:

> "It is of great importance that you **READ THIS LIST VERY CAREFULLY**. It will help you to understand our Community and why things happen the way they do inside of it, who leaves, and why.
> **GAD** = *GOOD FORTUNE*: People who possess this nature will have all their concentration placed on money. **They will not stay,** for the Devil (CH) will succeed in making them rich.
> **SIMEON** = *HEARING*: People who hear the truth, yet, still insist on **going to other so-called "Muslim communities".**
> **LEVI** = *JOINED:* **People who will leave** the "Truth" and join those communities which cater to their selfish desires and egos."

Jess Cagle - "So although they're free to leave the compound at any time, they are paralyzed with fear."

Fact - Compound? Okay, a compound is a fenced or walled-in area containing a group of buildings and especially residences. Jess Cagle attempts to paint a picture of barbed wire fences surrounding the community. This is false. There were no barriers that enclosed the Nuwaupian's place of residence. There was an Egyptian Pylon "entrance way" [pictured on the next page] with a security guard that monitored and controlled the flow of traffic.

Remember when Niki said *"We had security guards to guard people from not coming on to the Property, but we were not behind a gate with a lock-and- key."* This is a picture confirming there is no gate with a lock-and-key nor a barrier or wall that encloses. Here is another view of the entrance gate or Pylon to the left and the street 142 Highway in Eatonton, Georgia.

This is not by far a compound in the "group of buildings enclosed by a barrier" with barbed wires pictured below that "People Magazine" and the likes would like to plant in your mind of Dr. York and Nuwaupians. This picture below is not by far how the Community that Dr. York and Nuwaupians lived in looked.

Ruby - *"When I left I was crying because this was some place I thought I could live the rest of my life and it would be better than, you know, everything out here. As I'm going down hill rolling out to the gates, I thought about the little girl. I said, I left her there, what's gonna happen to her and who else he's doing stuff to?...I was riddled with guilt. I just felt detached from everything, you know, from reality."*

Fact - Wait a minute...Just wait a minute...You left the community correct? Okay. You were sane enough to leave the community correct? Okay. You were not paralyzed with fear to the point where you couldn't leave; correct? Okay. You felt detached from everything and reality; correct? Okay. You were riddled with guilt; correct? Okay. So now; While feeling detached from everything and riddled with guilt; throughout all of that; You had enough sanity to leave, HOWEVER not enough sanity to think enough about the well-being of a little girl being sexually abused??? To condone why you didn't report this alleged incident, you say you were detached from everything and reality; correct? BUT you were not so detached from reality that YOU YOURSELF couldn't and didn't know how to leave or walk away; correct? We don't doubt that you were detached from reality; And that reality you were and are detached from is the fact that Dr. Malachi Z. York never committed these sick acts that you allege he did.

Sheriff Sills - *"The first information that York was molesting children came to me from medical professionals in the area who finally felt obligated to tell me that very young women that came from the Nuwaubian Compound was having babies."*

Fact - Sills says the info came to him from medical professionals in the area. What area? On the land in the Community or medical professionals outside the community? Sills says these medical professionals finally felt obligated to tell him that *"very young women"* from the Nuwaupian Community were having babies. This implies that these medical professionals concealed and withheld information of a criminal nature and then later revealed it to Sills. Why didn't Sills say that these *"very young women"* were being impregnated by Dr. York? Furthermore, why didn't Sills say minors who were from the Nuwaupian Community were having babies by Dr. York? The answer is simple because no minor was ever found to be pregnant by Dr. York, let alone molested.

"These charges arose out of an investigation conducted by Putnam County, Georgia law enforcement officials, the Federal Bureau of Investigation (FBI) and the Internal Revenue Service (IRS). The Petitioner (Dr. York) was allegedly the leader of a religious organization, initially named the Nubian Islaamic Hebrews, that was deemed a cult by the FBI, prompting the instant investigation. <u>In 1998 [1997], law enforcement officials started receiving anonymous letters and e-mails stating that sexual misconduct was occurring on the Petitioner's [Dr. York] Property in Eatonton, Georgia.</u>"

[Case 5:02-CR-00027-CAR Document 382 Filed 6-27-07]

So Law Enforcement Officials were aware that Sexual Misconduct was occurring on the Nuwaupian Community circa 1998 A.D. and they were so concerned about the children and devoted to their legal responsibility to serve and protect the well-being of the those being sexually abused on "The Land" that they promptly and responsibly responded 5 years later on May 8, 2002 A.D. because they cared so much about the lives of those being abused by this man who had no history of these heinous acts, right?

Narrator - *"The turning point for the investigation comes when Sheriff Howard Sills gets a call from Dwight York's son, Jacob, who left the cult a decade earlier after becoming disillusioned with his father's teachings."*

Fact - Oh what a tangled web People Magazine weaves when their sources are those who deceive. We already know The Master Teacher is properly titled **Dr. Malachi Z. York**, so that's clear. We want to thank you for bringing up Jacob because you will know the truth and the truth is not what "People Magazine" have been telling you. Jacob was born July 11, 1973 A.D. as Yaquwb Abdullah Muhammad to the union of the late Dorothy Johnson aka Dhubayda and Dr. York. Jacob "Jake"(Pictured below far left) grew up in the community in Brooklyn, New York.

Jacob "Jake" did not leave the community because he became disillusioned with Dr. York's teachings. **Jacob was put out of the Community for having sex with little boys; The very acts he accuses Dr. York of. Jacob York is the CHILD MOLESTER and NOT Dr. York!!!**

Jacob's brewing hatred of Dr. York has been kindling for years. Jacob's mother "Dhubayda" passed away from a brain aneurysm to which Jacob blames Dr. York for and has even vowed vengeance against Dr. York. When Jacob left the community he got involved with the "Hip-Hop" world. He was the associative executive producer of Lil Kim's first album "Hard Core." Just do a google search of "Hard Core" - Lil Kim's first album and you will see him listed as such. Jacob's hate for Dr. York increased when Jacob came to Dr. York for some money hoping Dr. York would help him back Lil Kim. Dr. York refused to support Jacob in his endeavors because he did not want Lil Kim and her content of music to reflect back on the modest principles of The Nuwaupian Community. It is important at this time that we present a **portion** of Dr. York's Musical Résumé to show the extent of his influence in the Hip-Hop Community in his efforts to reach the young generation with uplifting messages to keep them off the path of Self-Destruction.

DR. YORK'S INFLUENCE

Dr. York in 1985 A.D. below performing his song **"It's on me"** while on stage for British Television. Dr. York proudly displaying the six pointed star and crescent of the Ansaaru Allah Community on his chest.

POSDNUOS (ball-head Nubian man positioned above Dr. York's right shoulder) from the Hip-Hop group **DE LA SOUL** sitting down listening to Dr. York teach on the Land in Eatonton, Georgia.

Posdnuos gives a shout out to Dr. Malachi Z. York and The Holy Tabernacle Ministries in the liner notes of **DE LA SOUL'S** 1996 A.D. Album - **Stakes Is High (pictured on the next page)**

Posdnuos (pictured on the next page on left) in the liner notes of **DE LA SOUL'S** 1996 A.D. C.D. - **Stakes Is High** says in the last sentence "Divine Love to Dr. Malachi Z. York and the Holy Tabernacle Ministries."

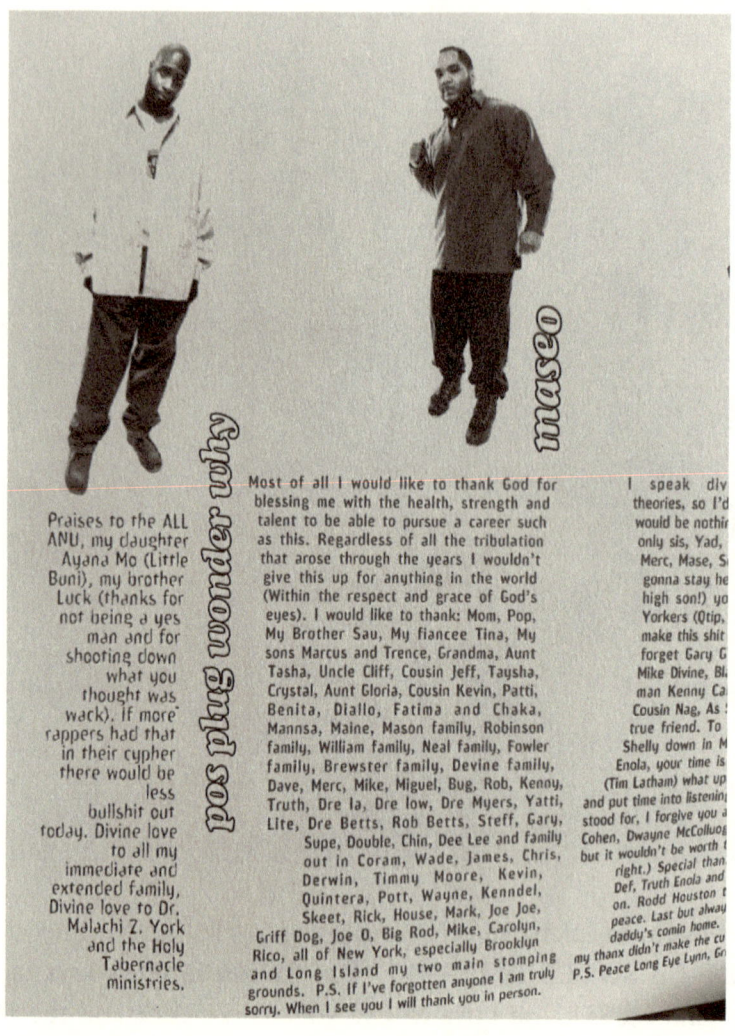

Lord Shafiyq from the Hip-Hop group **The Chosen Ones** proudly displaying the Six-pointed Star & Crescent symbol of Dr. York's community - The Ansaaru Allah Community. Lord Shafiyq in the Song entitled *"The Chosen Ones"* gives a shout out to Dr. York and I quote *"Elijah Muhammad, the brother is chosen, Marcus [Garvey] and Farrakhan are chosen* **and my Teacher Imaam Issa [Dr. York]** *is definitely chosen."*

Biographical Rebuttal To People Magazine

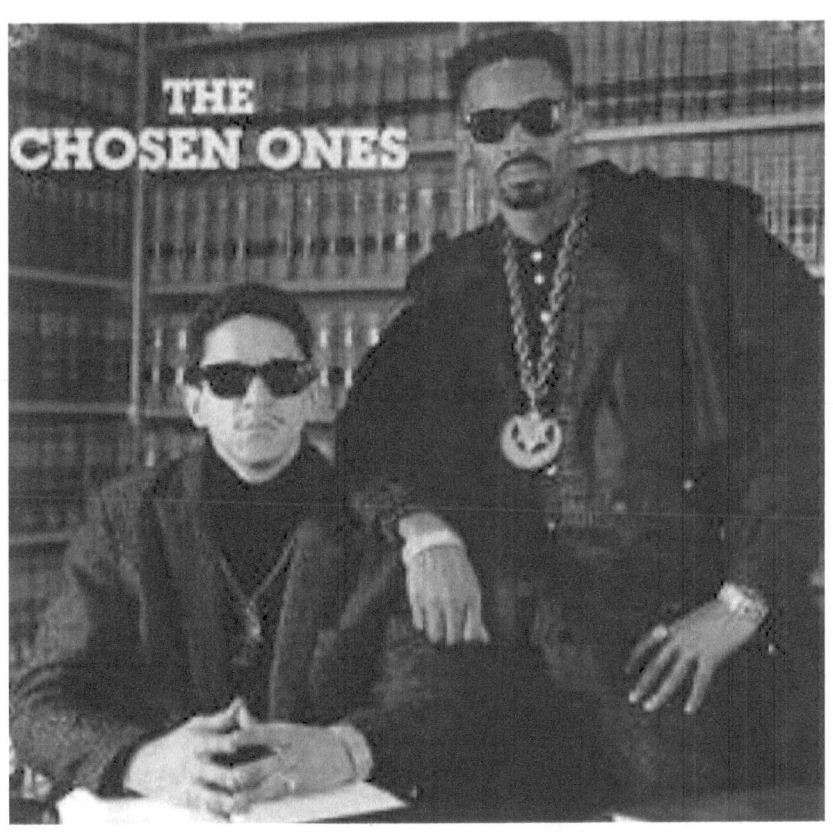

For anyone asking **"Does Dr. Malachi Z. York try to hide the fact that he was Imaam Issa?"** The answer is simply NO, and he even wrote a book with the same title to clear and address the skeptics and slanderers which is pictured below:

Hip-Hop Artist **Redhead Kingpin** of **Redhead Kingpin and the F.B.I.** is shown wearing the **"Nubian Flag"** medallion of the Ansaar Allah Community right above his Africa pendant.

This is an enlarged photo of the Nubian Flag medallion below:

One of, if not THE Greatest Hip-Hop group of all time **Public Enemy** mentioned The Ansaar Community in the liner notes of one of, if not THE Greatest Hip-Hop Album of all time **FEAR OF A BLACK PLANET** (pictured below).

········ BIOGRAPHICAL REBUTTAL TO PEOPLE MAGAZINE ········

In the liner notes of **Public Enemy's - FEAR OF A BLACK PLANET** C.D. under **Influential Inspirations**: "The Ansaar Community" is mentioned on the 6th line (pictured below).

INFLUENTIAL INSPIRATIONS:
Muhammad Ali, Muatta Kentatta, Bob Law, FOI, Minister Louis Farrakhan, Nation of Islam, Dick Gregory, Rev. Jesse Jackson, Black Panther Party, Dr. Frances Cress Welsing, Dr. Ivan Van Sertima, Don Cox, Lisa Williamson, Sister of Instruction, Director of Attitude, Ansaar Community, Steve Coakley, Geronimo Pratt, Last Poets, Gary Byrd, Leonard Muhammad Farrakhan, Mark Riley, Sister Ava Muhammad, Richard Pryor, Stevie Wonder, Rev. Charles Williams, Dr. Khalid Muhammad

LYRICAL INSPIRATION:
Daddy O (Stetsasonic), Kane, Melle Mel, L.L. Cool J, Kool Moe Dee, Willie Dee Rakim, KRS-One

SHOW INSPIRATION:
Run-D.M.C.

To my brothers The Ghetto Boys and The Soldier of the Highest Degree, Ice T; This one's from me Chuck D

Dedication to the memory of Brother Huey P. Newton, Keith (Cowboy) Wiggins, Yusef Hawkins and Oliver X. Beasley-Brothers from 4 different generations whose early departures from this planet symbolized the continuing conspiracy to destroy the Black male by murder, drugs and disease

SPECIAL THANKS:
Russell Simmons, Lyor Cohen, Everyone at Rush Artists Management and Def Jam Recordings

PUBLIC ENEMY MERCHANDISE: P.E. Merchandise
Asiatic Dept. A-1
510 S. Franklin St.
Hempstead, N.Y. 11550

PUBLIC RELATIONS & SPECIAL PROJECTS: Harry Allen
Hip-Hop Activism & Media Assa
c/o Community Research Instit
GPO Box 7718
New York, N.Y. 10116
Dept. BP-1

PUBLIC ENEMY INFORMATION: Dept. PE-7
510 S. Franklin St.
Hempstead, N.Y. 11550

HISTORICAL BOOK LIST INFORMATION AND PERSONAL SITUATIONS: Dept. S-1
510 S. Franklin St.
Hempstead, N.Y. 11550

LECTURE CIRCUIT INFORMATION: Dept. LC-19
510 S. Franklin St.
Hempstead, N.Y. 11550

PUBLIC ENEMY BLACKLINE: 1-900-HOT-PETV
1-900-468-7388
FEATURING 1) NEWS AND INFO IN THE RAP WORLD
2) FLAVOR FLAV LAMPIN' LINE
3) NATIONAL NUBIAN NEWS NETWORK
GET IT GOIN' ON!

"BLACK POWER 1990 IS A COLLECTIVE MEANS OF SELF DEFENSE AGAINST THE WORLDWIDE CONSPIRACY TO DESTROY THE BLACK RACE. IT'S A MOVEMENT THAT ONLY PUTS FEAR IN THOSE THAT HAVE A VESTED INTEREST IN THE CONSPIRACY, OR THAT THINK THAT IT'S SOMETHING OTHER THAN WHAT IT ACTUALLY IS...."

"UNITED WE STAND, YES DIVIDED WE FALL TOGETHER WE CAN STAND TALL ..."
"BROTHERS GONNA WORK IT OUT"

Hip-Hop legend **Doug E. Fresh** wearing "**A Proud Nubian**" Black-Red-and-Green-Flag of the Ansaaru Allah Community sweatshirt distributed by the Ansaar Allah Community in Brooklyn, New York.

Grandmaster Melle Mel & Van Silk in the video *"What's the matter with your world"* Grandmaster Melle Mel proudly displays the "Nubian Flag" of the Ansaaru Allah Community below on his left breast all throughout the video entitled *"What's the matter with your world"*

Hip-Hop group **KMD** had a video entitled *"Peach Fuzz"* In the beginning of the video you see the group with a table displaying books, posters and other products distributed by the Ansaaru Allah Community. Behind KMD on the red-brick wall is the *"We Are Family"* poster which shows the Master Teacher Dr. Malachi Z. York in the middle and 12 other Leaders who have contributed to the upliftment of Nubians here in the West. At 3 minutes and 25 seconds Zev Love X says in a humorous shout out *"I eat no Pork so why can't I be as smooth as my man Dr. York."*

The SOURCE - Magazine of hip-hop music, culture & Politics had an article written by Akiba Solomon about Dr. Malachi Z. York and The Holy Tabernacle Ministries in its August 1997 edition on pg. 76. The article gives a "rough" nutshell synopsis of Dr. York, his teachings and a few hip-hop artists influenced throughout the years. A picture of Dr. York is shown as Maku (Chief) Black Thunderbird Eagle identifying with his Native American Tribe - The Yamassee Native American Moors of the Creek Nation.

BIOGRAPHICAL REBUTTAL TO PEOPLE MAGAZINE

The Holy Tabernacle Ministry

FAR FROM A COLLECTION OF ABSTRACT, NUTTY TEACHINGS, THIS RELIGIOUS MINISTRY HAS MORE THAN ITS SHARE OF SUPPORTERS AMONGST THE RAP RANKS

...es my members." In addition, Trafant takes ...teens to cultural events throughout the city and plays current records during youth meetings.

"We then have a discussion on the material, a method that will teach teens to think critically about the world around them. We try to teach them not to accept everything at face value, even the things we say."

The following evening I'm sitting with Kelly Lynn Jackson, a marketing coordinator at Epic Records and a member of Emmanuel Baptist Church. "One Sunday Rev. Trufant had the young adults come down to 'Come On Ride The Train' by the Quad City DJs. They were dancing, but he had a way of relating his sermon to this," Taking a sip of bottled water, her expression serious, she continues, "I think God puts all of us through different trials and tribulations. I was in a situation a few years ago where I was almost killed by my roommate. I believe God has a plan for me, because after that night I really should have been dead."

His Eminence, the Rev. Run

In a recent conversation with a New York City public school teacher (who wishes to remain nameless), he relates, "One of the things I've noticed about teenagers is that they lean on religion in times of trouble or hardship, yet they rarely know how to apply the teachings to their everyday existence."

Turning to the church in distressing times is a subject that 18-year-old Vanessa Rodriguez can relate to without trying. "When I got pregnant I felt like I was in a crisis situation and I needed guidance. I was unclear about a lot of things, and after I started going to church I felt a little bit better about myself." Having attended Grace Church in Brooklyn with her father, she says, "I know I haven't lived-up to the teachings—I've smoked pot, had pre-marital sex and given my parents problems—but I trust in God to direct me on the right path. There have been a few Sundays when I just feel like staying in bed, but I'm always glad I got up. In this life you have to work towards being a better person."

As a member of the New Mount Cavalry Church in her home turf of Los Angeles, raptress Yo-Yo clearly understands the paradox of being "a child of God" and a provocative entertainer.

If you **overstand** that 4,004 years ago Zuen, a reptilian from the planet Titan, put the Spell of Sleep on the children of Eloheem Anunnaqu, thus creating the confusion, negativity and violence of Nubians today, then you've already been exposed to the Holy Tabernacle Ministry's (HTM) Right Knowledge scroll.

But don't write off HTM's doctrine as some old X-Files skit just yet. De La Soul, the Gravediggaz (minus the RZA), Stetsasonic and Born Jamericans didn't when they performed at the 1996 HTM Family Reunion. De La's Posdnuos even sent out "Divine love to Dr. Malachi Z. York and the Holy Tabernacle Ministries," in the liner notes of their latest project, *Stakes Is High*. The Dr. York that Pos mentioned is the "Reformer" and "Master-Teacher of the Truth And Facts For This Day," according to HTM literature. But to truly overstand the tenets of HTM, you must first understand its founder.

Dr. York was born in 1945 in the Sudan. Said to be a direct descendant of "the last prophet of the Muslim world," he arrived in the US as a child and went on to become an Islamic Imam at age 25. After the sighting of a comet called Bennet, which signaled the opening of the "Seventh Seal," York formed the Ansaar Allah Community in the West. A few years later, he and his followers became The Nubian Islaamic Hebrews.

At age 40, Dr. York revealed himself to be Melchizedek, the Angelic Being Michael (cited in Daniel 12:1 of the New Testament), whose purpose here on Earth is to spread the Ancient Mystic Order Of Melchizedek—otherwise known as the Holy Tabernacle. To this end, York founded the Holy Tabernacle Ministry in 1992. Throughout his career he has published over 360 pocket sized scrolls, translated and published several ancient texts, started an HTM university in Eatonton, Georgia, and constructed a language called Nuwaubic. York is even rebuilding the Temple of Solomon on Mt. Paran, a tract of HTM-owned land in Georgia.

"Dr. York actually used [the word] Nuwaubu in 1968, but the science was too deep for the mentality of the world that we had to master the religion first," explains Howard University chapter president Tony McEachern. "He had to cloak it in religion, and when it was time he brought it out in full."

Victor Felix, a founding member of the Howard chapter and of Nuwop Lon HTM-based hiphop collective), emphasizes that the Holy Tabernacle Ministry is not a religion. "It is a fra-

Dr. Malachi Z. York, founder of The Holy Tabernacle Ministry

ternal order. We deal in 360 degrees of the physical and 360 degrees of the spiritual—720 degrees of knowledge," he says after a marathon Right Knowledge Fellowship.

"720 degrees of knowledge?" you may wonder. But this divergence from standard geometric thought is minor compared to some of HTM's more unorthodox "facts." For example, according to York's teachings, the three major organized religions—Christianity, Islam and Judaism—are based on purposely mistranslated Holy Texts. And Dajaal, an extra-terrestrial, cast down to "Qi" [Earth] as a punishment for his egotism, spearheaded this religious conspiracy to deceive the children of Eloheem [Nubians]. And Jesus' real name is Y'shua. And through grammatical trickanology, "The Evil One" has the Muhammadaan [Muslim] world worshipping fire. Toni Ford, an occasional attendee of the Right Knowledge Fellowships, stresses that folks must consider these "facts" within the context they are presented. "Otherwise they do sound crazy," she says.

Although its teachings may seem daunting, the folks who study the ministry are not. "There are well over one million believers worldwide," says McEachern. "You can find them on the internet; and they own stores, stands and lodges in Chicago, Cleveland, Philadelphia, New York, D.C., New Jersey, North and South Carolina and Florida."

In fact, many HTM members are also one with the rhyme: McEachern says a group of HTM college students are pushing for the adoption of hip-hop as the official music of the Nuwaubic Nation. "HTM is for anyone who seeks the truth" says McEachern. "Whether they're Nubian or not."

AKIBA SOLOMON

Dr. Malachi Z. York in reference to his involvement in the Music Business said in a **True Light Audio-tape No. 82 entitled Diynu Allah/Diynul Islaam** and I quote: *"I accepted the slander and went into the music world, Why? Because I saw that Marvin Gaye reached more people on 1 record then every Imam (Leader) in the whole world did by giving a sermon on Friday."*

Billboard Magazine wrote an article about Dr. York in **the May 1985 issue written by Bobby Bennett and Jimmy Smith** which says in part and I quote:

"In the music business, I have come in contact with a lot of tremendously talented people, which is of course, no surprise. <u>The surprise is to come across a man like Dr. York, who is gifted in many different facets of this business and others. My partner and I both agree that never before have we encountered such a person.</u>"

Entire article from **Billboard Magazine** below.

Rare 1988 Promo display Ad below highlighting Dr. York's state of the art recording studio, artists and New additions to York records.

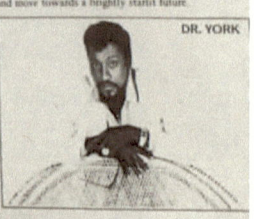

Below is a British Hip-Hop group called **The Scientists of Sound**. As you can clearly see the six pointed star and crescent of the Ansaaru Allah Community aka The Holy Tabernacle is worn around the necklace of the Scientist in the middle. In their song entitled "Like A Scientist" they say and I quote, *"Peace to my brothers* **The Nubian Islaamic Hebrews Ansaaru Allah**."

Spiritual Hip-Hop group **The Lost Children of Babylon** pictured on the next page dedicated a video to Dr. York entitled "**Martial Law**" with the caption "**A Political Prisoner wrongly imprisoned by the Federal Government**"

Below is the picture at the beginning of their video:

Kobina is Ghanaian and means born on Tuesday as June 26, 1945 A.D. (Dr. York's birthday) was on a Tuesday. **The Lost Children of Babylon** in front of the Black Pyramid on The Nuwaupian Community in Eatonton, Georgia.

Hip-Hop artist **Jaz-O** in the Originators video featuring **Jay-Z** is gowned in the attire of The Ansaaru Allah Community in 1990 A.D. Around 2 minutes and 50 seconds in the video you see Jaz-O with another brother proudly displaying Dr. York's portrait in his custom Sudanese white Garb.

Hip-Hop artist **Twista** in his song *"Say What"* off his 1992 A.D. Album **Runnin' Off at da Mouth** pictured below says and I quote: *"To the Ansaars in Chicago I say peace. To* **Dr. York** *and Abdul Malik I say peace."*

Heavy Mentalist **Killah Priest** mimics a similar pose of a picture that was drawn of Dr. Malachi Z. York on his album cover **"The Psychic world of Walter Reed"**

Below is the drawing of Dr. York that Killah Priest was mimicking.

Killah Priest in his song *"Looking Glass"* off his album **Behind the Stained Glass** says and I quote: *"And there was <u>Dr. Malachi Z. York</u> with deep thought, Called himself The Lamb, The Nuwaupian Godly Man, Built his own Egypt on the top of the sand."*

The late and great **Prodigy** pictured below (left in blue & white hoody and baseball cap) was very vocal in his support of Dr. Malachi Z. York's innocence and the influence Dr. York had on him.

In a YouTube video entitled **Was Prodigy killed because of the Facts he revealed about Dr. Malachi Z. York?** Prodigy is asked by an interviewer and I quote:

Interviewer - *"What woke you up to the New World Order of these Globalist elites and Eugenicists?"*

Prodigy - *"The main thing that woke me up to it was a writer named Dr. York a Spiritual teacher from Brooklyn. He had a whole Community over in Bushwick on Bushwick Avenue called the Ansaarullah.... That's how I learned reading his books and it all came from him."*

The late and great James Ingram dedicated a song to the Nuwaupian Community entitled "Tama-re [Sweet Golden City]" which he performed on Tama-re in 2001 A.D. which was the name of the Nuwaupian Community in Eatonton, Georgia. Here is a picture of James Ingram below wearing his Tama-Re T-Shirt next to Dr. Malachi Z. York.

Afrika Bambaataa - Pioneer and Godfather in the hip-hop world doesn't hide the fact that he was taught, influenced and supports the Innocence of Dr. Malachi Z. York. Afrika Bambaataa's **Return To Planet Rock** Album cover featuring **Jungle Brothers** which Dr. York was Executive Producer of shows the Nubian Flag on the lower left of the album as well as the Crystal City **(The Book of Revelation Chapter 21:11 ("...clear as crystal.")** known as the Mothership that is coming to collect the 144,000 worthy souls. [Pictured below at the end of Bambaataa's sword]

Afrika Bambaataa is pictured below in front of the Black Pyramid on Tama-Re with members of The Universal Zulu Nation and says the following in regards to the Imprisonment of Dr. Malachi Z. York:

"This is definitely a case that needs to be open, It needs to be open for all the public to see, for all the public to view, for the public to get an understanding so we can get the Right Knowledge, the Right Wisdom and the Right Overstanding on what has happened to our brother Dr. Malachi Z. York and <u>IF THIS CAN HAPPEN TO HIM, JUST IMAGINE WHAT CAN HAPPEN TO YOU."</u>

Afrika Bambaataa who supports the innocence of Dr. Malachi Z. York just so happened to be accused of the very same acts of child molestation that Dr. Malachi Z. York was falsely accused of. What was equally shocking was how quick the so-called Conscious Community easily accepted the allegations against Afrika Bambaataa. Even more shocking than the mentality of the so-called Conscious Community was the position of the so-called Conscious Elders in Hip-Hop who being well aware of the "Cointelpro" Element in Hip-Hop didn't even bother to mention the Cointelpro factor in Afrika Bambaataa's case. The Counter Intelligence Program was created by the FBI to **discredit** and **neutralize** specific individuals who were deemed potential Messiah's and groups considered revolutionary by the establishment. Informants infiltrated these groups for that purpose to cause chaos and dissention.

Question: Was Afrika Bambaataa's continued support of the innocence of Dr. Malachi Z. York dangerous to the Cointelpro objectives?

Answer: Yes. The FBI Cointelpro had a memo dated August 25, 1967 A.D. which said in part: "...*No political activist or somebody with an ideology that was perceived as a threat to the establishment should have access to a mass communication media.*" Afrika

Bambaataa has access to a *mass communication media* and his *ideology* which is in support of Dr. York's ideology of doing for self and independence which was echoed by many great Leaders of the past to Nubians here in the West; was and is perceived as a threat to the establishment. Cointelpro's purpose is to **discredit** and **neutralize**. What better way to discredit Afrika Bambaataa and neutralize his movement? Have Hip-Hop artists been the target of Cointelpro tactics in the past? Yes. But, also bear in mind that it is a known fact that there is **a special unit that exists inside of the New York Police Department devoted to Hip-Hop artists**. According to Cedric Muhammad former General Manager of the WU-TANG CLAN; **Sources revealed to him that individuals arrested on certain charges in New York City were being offered less time if they would say said charges were being done on behalf of the WU-TANG CLAN. It is also a known fact that the FBI, DEA and Local Houston Police Department had Rap-A- Lot Records CEO James Prince and Rapper Scarface under surveillance with approximately 400 informants planted in the 5th Ward Community!** Congressional Hearings on the Drug Enforcement Agency's (DEA) investigation of Rap-A-Lot Records revealed that it was difficult to "infiltrate the 5th Ward" and that no progress was made from 1992 A.D. - 1997 A.D. **until the Government began recruiting informants in the 5th Ward and Inside of the Rap-A-Lot Organization!** How soon the "Conscious Community" forgets.

Sheriff Sills - *"Jacob York wanted to meet with me to tell me what was really going on."*

Fact - So Jacob York met with the Sheriff Sills to tell him what was really going on and Jacob York wasn't at Dr. York's 2004 A.D. Trial? Why didn't the prosecution put Jacob York on the stand? Because the Government knew that under cross-examination the truth would come out that Jacob was on the FBI payroll to recruit people to testify against Dr. York because of the Bank Fraud that Jacob York was involved in which the Feds used against Jacob

York as leverage to solicit and compel disgruntled ex-members against Dr. York. This was an easy position for Jacob York to be in because of the hate he harbors for Dr. York. Two witnesses that testified at Dr. York's Trial in 2004 A.D. to the fact that Jacob York was on the FBI payroll to recruit others against Dr. York were Damon Pryor (Jacob's friend) and Leah Mabry (Jacob's sister). Damon Pryor's testimony was blocked from being admitted and heard by the Trial Jury. After Damon Pryor gave his testimony to Judge Charles Ashley Royal, Judge Royal said, **"NONE OF THAT'S ADMISSIBLE."** Below is his testimony by **Direct Examination by Adrian Patrick WITHOUT the Jury present.**

Adrian Patrick - *"Now if you would please, did you ever have a conversation with Jacob York concerning this case?"*
Damon Pryor - *"Yes"*
Adrian Patrick - *"All right. Were these one conversation or several conversations?"*
Damon Pryor - *"There were several conversations, but one main conversation that stands out in my mind."*
Adrian Patrick - *"All right. And what was the month and year of that conversation?"*
Damon Pryor - *"November 2001."*
Adrian Patrick - *"What did Jacob say?"*
Damon Pryor - *"He came to my house. It was the end of November, and the main gist of the conversation was."*
Adrian Patrick - *"Hold on just a second. Your Honor, do you want me to get into some of the background as to why he came and things? Do you want to know those type things?"*
Judge Charles Ashley Royal - *"Yeah"*
Adrian Patrick - *"All right. What was the reason, to your knowledge, why Jacob, what was the reason for the meeting?"*
Damon Pryor - <u>*"Well, Initially, it was for a favor. He [Jacob York] asked me to perform a duty he wanted done with bank statements that he had, and that was the initial meeting, for him to come to*</u>

the house and that we would talk about it and see what he wanted, What he requested."
Adrian Patrick - *"He wanted you to manipulate some bank statements?"*
Damon Pryor - *"Right; bank statements he wanted me to change or alter."*
Adrian Patrick - *"And for the Court's information, why would he come to you about that?"*
Damon Pryor - *"Because of my past criminal charge that I had with bank fraud, and he knew I was able to forge certain paperwork, so he asked me to do it."*
Adrian Patrick - *"Okay. That's the reason. Who set up the meeting with you all?"*
Damon Pryor - *"Christopher Cornelius, And I did, And Jacob York."*
Adrian Patrick - *"All right. Now, so he came to your home and what was the - - just try to get to - - what was the conversation related to this case?"*
Damon Pryor - *"Well, he [Jacob York] told me they had set up Pops (Dr. York) and that he (Dr. York) was going down. He said the girls that he was involved with, they came together and decided, through whatever reasons he had, that Pops was going down and he had it set up already. He said, "I will see it."*
Adrian Patrick - *"All right. Who were the girls he was talking about?"*
Damon Pryor - *"Adah ["Niki" Nicole Lopez], Abigail [Habibah Washington] and Atiyah. Those are the main ones that came up in the conversation."*
Adrian Patrick - *"All right. That's it, Your Honor."*
Judge Charles Ashley Royal - **"NONE OF THAT'S ADMISSIBLE"**
[January 20, 2004 A.D. Trial Testimony Case 5:02-CR-27-CAR]

Leah Mabry was the other Defense Witness for Dr. York; like Damon Pryor, Leah Mabry gave her testimony without the Jury present. After Judge Charles Ashley Royal heard her testimony he disallowed Leah Mabry to talk about her conversations between Jacob and herself with the Jury present. Leah Mabry's testimony - Direct Examination by Adrian Patrick WITHOUT the Jury present and WITH the Jury present is provided below:

(JURY NOT PRESENT)
Adrian Patrick - *"What's your relationship to Jacob York?"*
Leah Mabry - *"He's my brother"*
Adrian Patrick - *"All right. And did you ever have a conversation with him—well, you had several conversations with him?"*
Leah Mabry - *"A few, yes"*
Adrian Patrick - *"But one of the more recent conversations you had with him in relationship to this case, what was the nature—first of all, where did you all meet?"*
Leah Mabry - *"This was in Stone Mountain, Georgia."*
Adrian Patrick - *"Okay. And who was present?"*
Leah Mabry - *"My sister did drive me to his house, and a few of the—like Adah ["Niki" Nicole Lopez] was available, Atiyah—"*
Adrian Patrick - *"That's Atiyah Thomas?"*
Leah Mabry - *"Yes. Atiyah Thomas, Arlene Hamilton, And also David—"*
Adrian Patrick - *"David Noel?"*
Leah Mabry - *"Yes. David Noel and his mother"*
Adrian Patrick - *"Barbara Noel?"*
Leah Mabry - *"Yes. <u>Barbara Noel ["Niki's" Mom]</u> was available, also."*
Adrian Patrick - *"What was the conversation?"*
Leah Mabry - *"He wanted me to go to the FBI. He told me that things was already set up, that all I had to do was talk to the FBI and tell them that I was molested by Mr. York."*
Adrian Patrick - *"All right"*
Judge Charles Ashley Royal - *"Well, what did he specifically tell you? What were his words?"*
Leah Mabry - <u>*"He told me that things was already set up by the FBI and that all I had to do was speak to them."*</u>
Adrian Patrick - *"Your Honor, again, I'm emphasizing the ongoing enterprise here. Even though the semantics show that something was*

set up, it's indicating an entity that is an ongoing enterprise, from him speaking with his sister, saying, "All you have to do is speak with the FBI" to speaking with Damon Pryor saying, "He's going down, you'll see." The semantics of the words "is already set up" Your Honor, only indicates the point that there's an ongoing enterprise."

Leah Mabry - "Yes. May I add that he also told me that he was on a PAYROLL BY THE FBI and that I could also be added onto the same payroll."

[Following the Prosecutions cross examination; Judge Charles Ashley Royal chimes in and says]

Judge Charles Ashley Royal - "Okay, I understand that there are basically two components to what she wants to say, "things are already set up by the FBI and all she had to do was speak to them."

Leah Mabry - "Yes."
Judge Charles Ashley Royal - "I FIND THAT THE FIRST PART OF THAT IS INADMISSIBLE. However, she can testify to the second part of that, that she was told by her brother that all she had to do was speak to the FBI."
Adrian Patrick - "Your Honor, can there be—well, can there be testimony as to an explanation of why he said that, though?"
Judge Charles Ashley Royal - "NO"
(JURY PRESENT)
Adrian Patrick - "How are you doing, Ms. Mabry?"
Leah Mabry - "Doing good."
Adrian Patrick - "How old are you?"
Leah Mabry - "23"
Adrian Patrick - "All right. And, Ms. Mabry, how long have you been a member of the organization with Malachi York?"
Leah Mabry - "23 years"
Adrian Patrick - "All right. Were you born into the organization?"
Leah Mabry - "Yes, I was"

Adrian Patrick - *"Do you have a brother named Jacob York?"*
Leah Mabry - *"I do, yes."*
Adrian Patrick - *"And is Malachi York your father?"*
Leah Mabry - *"Yes, he is."*
Adrian Patrick - <u>*"What type relationship does Jacob York have against Malachi York?"*</u>
Leah Mabry - <u>*"He has a vendetta against him. He hates him."*</u>
Adrian Patrick - *"Have you ever been molested by Malachi York?"*
Leah Mabry - *"Never"*
Adrian Patrick - *"Have you ever had a reason to go to law enforcement or FBI, or whatever, to report a molestation by Malachi York?"*
Leah Mabry - *"No, no reason at all."*
Adrian Patrick - <u>*"Have you ever— has it ever been suggested to you that you should go to the FBI?"*</u>
Leah Mabry - <u>*"Yes, by Jacob York."*</u>
Adrian Patrick - *"What was his statement to you?"*
Leah Mabry - <u>*"He told me I should go to the FBI and tell them I was molested by Malachi York."*</u>
Adrian Patrick - *"When did this take place?"*
Leah Mabry - *"In May of 2001."*
Adrian Patrick - *"Who was present or where was it at?"*
Leah Mabry - *"In Stone Mountain at a house he was living in. Atiyah was there, Atiyah Thomas, Nicole Lopez, and also her mother Barbara, and also David."*
Adrian Patrick - *"Hold on. Barbara Noel?"*
Leah Mabry - *"Yes. Barbara Noel And David Noel And Arlene Hamilton, and also Amala Noel."*
Adrian Patrick - *"So Amala Noel, David Noel, and Barbara, Atiyah Thomas, were at the home when Jacob York made the statement to you?"*
Leah Mabry - *"Yes."*
Adrian Patrick - *"No further questions."*

[January 20, 2004 A.D. Trial Testimony Case 5:02-CR-27-CAR]

<u>Judge Royal would not allow the testimony in that Jacob York is a paid informant for the FBI.</u>

Sheriff Sills - *"So I said fine, I'll meet with you [Jacob York] at the FBI Office in Atlanta at 9:00. We go into the FBI Office, he sits down in the Office with myself and FBI agents and begins to tell us the whole story of York, that he was routinely having sex with underage girls often; very underage girls, that he was on the 3rd generation of doing that with girls. <u>Then I basically said you know I want to talk to one of these women this happened to, He said sure one of them is in the car, I'll go get her now.</u>"*

Fact - *"One of these women"* that Sheriff Sills wanted to talk to was **Habiba "Abigail" Washington** - The prosecution's key witness in Dr. Malachi Z. York's 2004 A.D. Trial. Habiba "Abigail" Washington like "Niki" (Nicole Lopez) had an immunity agreement and I quote her Trial Testimony - **Direct Examination by Mr. Moultrie:**

Mr. Moultrie - *"Now, before I ask you any other question, I want you to tell the jury if you entered into an agreement between you and the Government that involved an immunity agreement."*
Habibah "Abigail" Washington - *"Yes, I did."*
Mr. Moultrie - *"And what did you understand your agreement to be with the government concerning that immunity agreement?"*
Habibah "Abigail" Washington - *"I understood it to mean that I was cooperating with the government and my testimony would not be used against me."*
Mr. Moultrie - *"And what did you understand your responsibility to be with respect to your testimony?"*
Habibah "Abigail" Washington - <u>*"To tell the truth."*</u>
 [January 12, 2004 A.D. Trial Testimony Case 5:02-CR-27-CAR]

However, Habibah Washington did **NOT** tell the whole truth concerning the charges against Dr. York during Dr. York's 2004 A.D. Trial according to her **Recant Video dated April 18, 2004**

A.D. she makes this clear when she says **"I just want to repeat that the charges brought up against Malachi were all lies."** Habibah Washington also did a **sworn written AFFIDAVIT April 23, 2004 A.D.** which exposed the Conspiracy against Dr. Malachi Z. York and I quote:

Affidavit of Habiybah Washington

1. I am 28 years of age and reside in Brooklyn, New York. I make this affidavit of my own free will. No one has threatened or coerced me to make it. Nor have I been offered anything of value in return for making this affidavit. I understand that in light of my previous testimony and my statements to Federal agents and an Assistant U.S. Attorney, **I can be prosecuted for perjury and other crimes. In spite of the risk I am putting myself in, I am prepared to make this affidavit in order to make up for my previous perjury.**

2. In May 2001, I had a conversation with Jacob York at his house. Also present were Nuh and Rashid. Jacob told me that I should go to the FBI with a story because there were rumors going around that some people were speaking to the FBI, that the FBI had my name, and they knew that I was in charge of the land [**Tama-re**] for some period of time. He said that there were rumors that some children were telling the FBI that they had been molested and that the kids mentioned my name and said that I knew about what was going on. He told me to go to the FBI first and that I should not wait for the FBI to come to me and ask me about it. I told him that I did not want to talk to the FBI and that I did not have any reason to talk to them. I told Jacob that I

did not have any knowledge that anything wrong was going on. **Jacob said that he wanted his father to go to jail, that his father did not deserve to live**, and that we could go to the land and kidnap all the little kids there so that nothing happens to them. I told Jacob that nothing was happening to the kids and nothing would happen to them. Jacob asked me to think about it, and the conversation ended.

3. On the way back from Florida, I had another conversation with Jacob, Farrah (names blacked-out) were also in the car. Jacob again proposed that we go to the land [**Tama-re**] to kidnap our little sisters and brothers. He again told me that I should go to the FBI and not wait for them to come to me with whatever they had on me because if I did not they could come after me. He said that whatever anyone said against me they could use against me. I believed him when he said that other people had gone to the FBI. He did not want to give me names (name blacked-out) and I were listening. **I told him that I did not want to tell a story against his father even though I was angry with Malachi.** I told him that things were not good between Malachi and me and that we were just arguing all the time. Jacob said that he heard that Pops had sex with (name blacked-out) and he wanted me to confirm that. **I told him that I never saw him have sex with any of these boys.** He asked me over and over again, and I told him that I did not know anything about it and that he should talk to whoever it was who was telling him these things. I kept on telling him that I did not know anything. **(Names blacked-out) were saying why they were angry with Malachi. Jacob said that he was living for the day when he would see his father in jail. I asked him why he was so angry with his father. He told me that he thought his father had mistreated his mother and had a lot to do with her death.** He said that his father

was a coward and that he really did not believe that he should be living.

4. After we got back from Florida, we stayed at Jacob's house. The next day, Jacob showed me a documentary about cults, Charles Manson, David Koresh, Jim Jones and a guy in California. I think his name was Marshall Applegate [Applewhite]. He asked me to compare all of these stories with the way we grew up. He said that his father [Dr. York] had grown up in the same way these guys had, that they had the same mentality, that we were a cult. The thought had never occurred to me before. I had mixed reactions. I told him that some of the comparisons with those groups made sense but that I still did not believe that we grew up in a cult. He said that I just didn't know that we grew up in a cult because we were living in it.

5. I tried to contact my sister, Islah, who was still living on the land. I felt I was getting the runaround from people on the land and at Athens. I told the lady whom I believed was giving me the runaround that if I couldn't talk to my sister, matters were going to get worse. I was very angry. I told Jacob about what had happened on the phone, and he said you see this is what we are dealing with. This is the reason why we have to put an end to this, you should just be able to go up to the land and take your sister. He brought up the kidnapping thing again, and I told him that I didn't want to kidnap her and that if she wanted to leave she should just leave on her own. We started talking about living upstate, and he asked me when I started having sex with his father. I told him that it was when I was 17. He said that he didn't believe me and that it would help me if I said that I was thirteen when we first started having sex.

6. I finally talked to my sister. She told me that my father had been kicked out and living on the streets. I was very angry with Malachi because of this, and I vented to Jacob. He told me that if I wanted to speak to the Sheriff, I could. I told him that I would talk to the FBI. He called the Sheriff and made arrangements. The next day Jacob and I went to the FBI Office.

7. **They interviewed Jacob first, and I stayed in the car. Then about an hour later they called me up and interviewed me. I told him that I had sex with Malachi when I was thirteen. That was false.** I had about four or five more interviews, possibly more. **During this time, I was comparing notes with (names blacked- out, However, the names will be given in Habiybah's Recantment Video). We stayed in touch by telephone and we told each other what happened in each of our interviews. For example, the FBI asked me if I remembered that there was a naked picture taken of (name blacked-out), I told them that I didn't remember. But then I spoke to (name blacked-out) and she told me that she had told them that. So the next time I met with the FBI, I told them that I remembered.**

8. In my initial interview, I told the FBI that for a period I had run the finances. They asked me how we kept our money and if we paid taxes. I explained to them everything about the finances. The first time structuring came up was when I interviewed in 2003 by IRS agents. I believe it was September or November of 2003. After the interview I called Jalaine, an FBI agent, and told her that I didn't understand the interview, that I didn't understand the purpose. I then had another interview with the IRS agents and Richard Moultrie. <u>**They asked if Malachi had ever told me not to sign reports. I told them No.**</u> One of them told me that (name blacked-out) had told them that he told her not to

sign them. I told them not say Malachi was an angel, but that (name blacked-out) said that to cover her ass because she's the one who actually gave the bank tellers a hard time. They said that it was a possibility that Malachi could have said it to her, but that as far as I knew he had never said it to me. They asked if we broke down deposits so that we didn't deposit more than ten thousand dollars. I told them, yes. They asked how I knew to do that. I told them that (name blacked-out) had explained to me how to do the finances. I do not remember if they asked me if Malachi knew about it.

9. **Malachi has never done the deposits with us. I do not know if he knew that we were breaking down the deposits. He never told me or, to my knowledge, anyone else not to deposit more than $10,000 at a time.**

10. During the interviews, the agents told me that I was doing the right thing, stay strong. <u>They also reminded me that I could be incriminated on a lot of the charges myself,</u> that I was doing this for the children, and that I was a victim myself. They said that the children needed me for this case, that I was the main witness.

11. **I was never molested by Malachi York.** I first had sex with him when I was seventeen years old and I did it voluntarily. He never forced me to have sex. <u>**I do not know of anyone he has ever molested. I do not know of any children he has ever had sex with. I never took any children to him for the purpose of sex.**</u> I did take children to his house to watch movies in his movie theaters and to play. He would have picnics with his children so he could spend time with them. I do not know if he has ever been involved in structuring of deposits or if he ever knew that we were doing it.

12. **My lawyer and Jonathan Marks, Malachi York's lawyer, have explained to me that I am putting myself at risk by signing this affidavit.** I know that, but I want the truth to come out. I do not believe that Malachi York should be in prison for crimes he did not commit.

[END OF HABIYBAH'S AFFIDAVIT]

Money was a motive in the case against Dr. Malachi Z. York. Habiybah Washington was told that she should write a book about Dr. York because it would make her money. Not only does Adrian Patrick reveal that Habiybah Washington was offered "favorable concessions" but the Prosecution (Richard Moultrie) lied and said that the offer of favorable concessions was nonexistent. The Trial transcripts reveal this and I quote her trial testimony Cross Examination by Adrian Patrick below:

Adrian Patrick - *"Ms. Washington sometimes you go by Gail correct?"*
Habibah "Abigail" Washington - *"Yes"*
Adrian Patrick - *"Isn't it true you had conversations about a movie or book related to this case?"*
Habibah "Abigail" Washington - *"No -- well, yes... I was asked should I write a book.... believe it was Derrick Hodges. -- He wanted me to write the book... he mentioned that if I was to do a book, you know, it would make a lot of money."*
Adrian Patrick - *"Isn't it true that you informed the Government that you would give testimony against the defendant in return for favorable concessions?"*
Mr. Moultrie - *"-- Your Honor, it doesn't say anything about favorable concessions. Those words are not going to appear in that document."*
Adrian Patrick - *"Would you [Habiybah] read the first sentence in that document?"*
Habibah "Abigail" Washington - [Reading] *"You have indicated that you are desirous of providing information to the government*

which would be of assistance in a criminal investigation and prosecution of others in return for "favorable concessions" to you."

[January 12, 2004 A.D. Trial Testimony Case 5:02-CR-27-CAR]

Habibah "Abigail" Washington's Recant Video dated April 18, 2004 A.D.

Preamble to Habiybah's Recant Video:

It is of utmost importance that you read and pay attention to Habiybah's words very carefully for she details and reveals the conspiracy against Dr. Malachi Z. York below:

Habiybah Washington Recant Video

"Hello, My name is Habiybah Washington and today **I'm here to put on record, the truth behind all of the lies brought up in the case against Malachi York.** I'm going to start by saying that I'm not being forced, threatened, coerced or pressured to do this tape. I am also going to state that, as you can tell, I'm not under any kind of influence, alcohol or drugs. I want to begin with all of the events that led up to the final verdict in the case against Malachi. I want to start off with how it started, where it started, when and the reason why.

I left the community in February of 2001 A.D. I moved from Georgia and I went to New York and lived with my family. **In about March of 2001 A.D, I was contacted by Jacob [York]. Jacob is the son of Malachi York; he's also an ex-member.** Jacob contacted me and our conversation was basically about the good times that we had in the community, what we went through, how we grew up, just making up for old times. Two months after that, Jacob called me. This was in May. Jacob called me about a trip to Florida, a trip where some the girls and boys, ex members that were going to go down to Florida, just to hang out, have fun, whatever. I agreed to go on the trip. I told Jake [Jacob] I'll come on the trip. I left from New York, went to Georgia, we all met up at Jacob's house. It was me, Jacob, Nicole Lopez [Niki], Nuh Rashid, Aiys, Istiyr, probably some other girls and boys, I don't remember.

Before we actually went down to Florida I had a conversation with Jacob outside of his house and Jacob brought up some feelings that he had about his father. Jacob was really upset with his father. He stated that he hated his father, that he felt that his father doesn't need to be alive, that he shouldn't even be given life. He felt that his father needs to just rot in jail. Jacob wanted all of us to, all of us meaning me, Nicole [Niki], Karima, he was talking to a couple of people, different people that left the community. He wanted us to bring a case against his father. Jacob told me that some of the girls and boys that left the community had went to the government about different things that was going on in the community, meaning child molestation. Before I left the community, I was the main person in charge of the finances, as well as in charge of anything that went on in the community. The living, eating, anything financial, anything that happened regarding any of the members in the community, I dealt with that, so I was basically in charge.

Jacob told me that the FBI knew who I was and that they were told about certain things that I've done in the community and some of those things I could be incriminated for. Jacob told me that if I don't go to the FBI first then they would come after me, they would incarcerate me, they would take my children away from me because there are things that they were told about me that could incriminate me.

When Jacob first talked to me about that, I was not interested in bringing out any charges against his father. I didn't see any reason. I didn't believe that anything was going on, I didn't believe that anything was wrong, we wasn't doing any criminal acts. Jacob brought up the fact that I had a son by his father at 17 years old. I told Jacob that my son with his father never came about because I was forced to have sex with his father. Yes I was seventeen years old and yes I did agree to have a child with his father at that age. I understood my age, I understood his age, I didn't see anything wrong with it, I consented to it, so I told Jacob that that's the way that I felt. I didn't feel that anything wrong happened. That we both agreed to it. I felt that I was an adult, it was my decision and I went with it.

But Jacob proceeded to say that there were some things that some of the other ex- members had went to the government with and that I should really talk to them and see what's up and see how I can clear my name so that I'm not prosecuted for any of those things.

We all went to Florida after that conversation and during our trip to Florida. We had several conversations in the car with Jacob. It was some other boys that were there and Jacob started talking about going on the land and taking some of the kids, just kidnapping some of the children off the land. He was talking about my sister, my sister was still there, my younger sister Islah was still there and he wanted us to just go up there and just take her and take some of the other little girls and boys off the land because he didn't feel that they should be living on the land with his father. But we had all agreed that that was not going to happen. None of us was interested in going up on the land and kidnapping anybody, so Jacob said, "Well then, we can just do it the legal way." He started bringing up different things in the community like how we grew up, how we lived. He [Jacob] brought up the fact that he was in love with Nicole and he felt that because Nicole liked his father that it was a betrayal and that his father was the one responsible for it. **Jacob thought that his dad was responsible for his mother's death and his brother's death and he really, really felt that he needed to take revenge on his father and he was not able to do it, but we were able to do it because we were there longer and we were closer to his dad than he was.** *So Jacob had a conversation with me and Karima and Nicole Lopez [Niki].* **Nicole Lopez [Niki] had a lot of disgruntled issues with Jacob's dad, because for one, she was kicked out and she felt that it was wrong that she was kicked out because she didn't have anywhere to go. She didn't know anybody and after all the years that she lived in the community, Malachi kicked her out, and she had nowhere to go. So she was kind of mad about that.** *Everybody started venting in the car about different things that we didn't like. It didn't have nothing to do with child molestation, it had nothing to do with any criminal acts, it was just different things, normal things that you don't like about growing up or, you know, we may have had* *an argument with Malachi here and there and we brought up the situation. Jacob kind of fed off of that anger and he convinced all of us that we should take that anger and we should go to the government with a story about his father.* We all went down to Florida and we had fun, we did our thing, on the trip back from Florida, we were driving in Jacob's car again. It was myself, Karima, Nicole, Farah, Nuh Rashid and some other driver I don't remember his name, and *Jacob brought up the conversation again, how he thinks that we should really go to the government with a story about his father.* Anything that we didn't like in the community we should go because his father needed to be in jail. His father did not do good things, he was not happy with his father and he really felt that a case should be brought up against his father. He really felt that his father should be put away for life. He did not deserve to live. That conversation subsided and we finally made it back to Georgia from Florida and *Jacob had a conversation with me again and he told me that there were certain children that did go to the FBI about different things with myself and that it was no way I would be able to prove that it didn't happen. The only way I can make any good of it is to go to the FBI with a story, seek immunity and just go from there.* I still told Jacob that I was not interested in doing that and there was nothing that I'd witnessed or nothing that I'd known that was going on, but Jacob believed that because the FBI knew who I was and because they were told things about me that it was best that I go to them and talk to them and see what's up.

    At that point I was afraid, I mean nobody really messes with the FBI. So I went to the FBI the following day. They called Jacob up first. I sat in the car. Jacob talked with them. I don't know what the conversation was about because I wasn't in the room and I wasn't told what the conversation was about, but Jacob went up there and he talked to them, and then about an hour later they called me up. *I stated my name. I stated who I was, they asked me about different children and they called out different names like Amala and Krystal, and I told them I know those children. Whatever name they called if I knew the person I told them I knew the person.*

········ BIOGRAPHICAL REBUTTAL TO PEOPLE MAGAZINE ········

They asked me to state my life, the reasons why I left and the reason why I was there. I told them about life in the community, growing up, why we left. I was questioned about the money situation because I did deal with the financial situation, I told them how we ran our finances, I ran off different people that I knew that was there, different people that I knew that had left and why they left. They asked me about certain children, they asked me about certain stories that they were told and I told them that yeah, I went along with the story, I told them that, "yes, I did do these things." I felt that I had to tell them yes because I was told that they already knew and there was no way for me to deny anything that didn't happen or anything that did happen. I had to tell them what I felt that they know because I felt that, like Jacob told me, they already knew the story and there was no way that I could say that didn't happen, I would have to prosecute myself, **to make whatever was said against his father, make it more real, make it sound more believable, if we all prosecuted ourselves then whatever we say about Malachi would be believable.** That interview ended by them asking me about different people that I knew that would want to talk, different members that I knew that would want to assist them in the case. The only names that I knew were other members that I knew that were disgruntled. Like Nicole had her own issues with Malachi, Karima had her own issues with Malachi, Sakina also, Amala, Krystal different people that I knew that had issues against him, I gave them those names.

So after that, they started calling different people. **Everybody kind of got involved. Everybody called everybody and that's how the case kind of started.** The question next would be, why did I go ahead with the story? Why did I never take it back? Why didn't I ever just tell the truth at that time?

I felt really pressured to go along with the story. I felt that I had to go along with the story. **We all kind of called each other and was backing up each other's story. If Nicole did an interview with the FBI then she would call us and we would back up her story. If Nicole spoke to them then she would call us so in case they called me, then I could back up whatever Nicole was saying and that's**

kind of how we did it. We all just called each other and said, "yeah, I did this, I said this" and then we can back each other up and that would make the story sound more real, make it sound more believable. *If we all back each other up, it can sound more believable. I was afraid that my initial interview that I had given a statement, I was afraid that if I was to take that back, I did not know if I was going to be prosecuted, it's not like I had an attorney to represent me. I did not have my personal attorney to explain to me what the steps were, what the charges were, what immunity really meant. What I believed immunity to mean was that I would be protected, anything that I would state on the witness stand that could be used against me, anything that I would say that could be used against me, I would be protected from that, that's what I understood my immunity to mean. It was never explained in detail what the agreement was about, what the immunity was about, that was the gist of what I understood it was about.* **So at the time, I went through with the story because I was afraid for my life, I was afraid they could take me to jail, that I could be incarcerated, that my children would be taken away from me, and it was different times during the two year process that I spoke to different FBI agents. I spoke to Joan [Cronier], I spoke to Jalaine [Ward], I spoke to Tracy [Bowen] from the Sheriff's department and there was a couple occasions where they did remind me that "you know Habibah you could be incriminated for certain things you are about to say as well." So being reminded of that, I felt compelled to just go ahead with the story, I didn't want to change my story at the time, I didn't want to break the agreement because I was told that by breaking the agreement meant that I would be incarcerated and I would be prosecuted because I had given statements already.** *And like I said, I wasn't represented by a personal attorney. The prosecution had an attorney that represented all the witnesses and all of the victims. I was not represented by a personal attorney. So, I really didn't know my rights, I really didn't know the laws, I didn't know what I could do, what I can't do, so I felt compelled to just go ahead with the story that everybody else was telling.*

Why I want to come out with the truth now? It's really, really important for me to come out with the truth now because I don't sleep at night knowing that two [Dr. York & Kathy Johnson at the time] people are spending their lives in jail as I speak because of statements that a bunch of ex-disgruntled members came out with. **The whole trial against Malachi was personal. It was on personal anger reasons. We all had our own issues why we were angry with him and Jacob told us that we could come out with a story, we could eventually file for a class action lawsuit, we could all sue him for millions of dollars and get money from it and we could even go to making movies and we could even go to making books and stuff like that. So everybody fed off of that idea.**

Prior to Jacob telling us about the civil suit, he showed us video documentary on Charles Manson, on the Heaven's Gate dude, different leaders that kind of ran cults and Jacob showed us this documentary. He showed it to me, showed it to Nicole, he basically showed it to everybody that left the community-the girls. And he wanted us to look at this documentary and compare it to his father. The way that we lived, the fact that, 'yes we did live with the children with the children, the parents with the parents, the brothers together, the mothers together.' He wanted us to compare everything that they've been through with us so that we can put in our minds that "no we didn't live a normal life, yes we were a cult" so he showed all of us that documentary so that we can sort of compare the two so that before we even start testifying, we could understand that yes we were a cult. He wanted that to be in our minds. So that we could go with that type of mind frame as opposed to "we were normal, we just all have our own issues, we're mad, but it's all good." No, he wanted us to believe that, "listen, this is the documentary on this cult and this is what we lived" and he wanted us to compare that so that we could have that type of mind frame. In other words, it added on to the anger that 'wow, this is how we grew up or this is what it is."

Anyways, like I was saying, **I feel totally guilty for bringing this case against Malachi. I don't feel that it's right that he is in jail right now because all of us were angry and we all got together**

and agreed to this case. And we went ahead with it and now he's facing life in jail for it. It's not right, it's not fair for anybody to be prosecuted because of somebody else's personal reasons. I don't think that he should be incarcerated because of that. If we all did have issues against him then that's human nature but nobody should be sent to jail because of a bunch of lies. And what was said on that stand was a bunch of lies. Like I said, we all called each other up we all backed each other's story up. We all kind of, 'okay you said this to this person and I said that to that person, okay that's fine.' Jacob went to each and every one of us and tried to make it personal between each and every one of us. *With me it was like "you was in charge, you had control of a lot of things and so anybody could say this about you and it would be believable because you was in charge." There was no denying that I was in charge, I was in charge. So I felt that I had to go along with the story because I couldn't prove anything that anybody would say against me. I couldn't prove it, he told me that once they told the FBI something, that the FBI is looking into you, they start looking into me. There was no way that I could prove that what anybody said about me wasn't the truth or wasn't a lie, there was no way, so I felt compelled to just go ahead with the story.* **As far as Nicole is concerned, Jacob appealed to her because Nicole was in love with one of the younger boys. And so Jacob knew that if they found out that about Nicole, Nicole would be so afraid that she didn't want to be incriminated for whatever feeling she had.** *So different people had different reasons. Jacob made everything personal between all of us. So we all had personal reasons for being pressured, or feeling that we had to go through with the story.*

Like I was saying, like Nicole Hardin, the whole situation with the RICO charges. **I know that I previously stated that Malachi York never told us to structure any money and he also never told us not to sign or not to report when we made over $10,000 dollars. He never told us not to ever file that report.** *In court, I was told Nicole Harden told the FBI that he did tell us not to sign that document, I would have known if he would have said that because*

I was in charge of the money. I was the person that was in charge of the financial office. *If anything was told about finances it would have definitely have come through me.* But I do believe that Nicole felt compelled to go ahead with that story because, for one, Nicole Hardin is the one who did refuse to sign those documents and she's also the one who always gave the tellers a problem and a hard time whenever it came to those types of transactions. So I believe that's the reason why Nicole did say that "yes, he said that." But he's never said that to me, he's never said that to anybody else that I've known, and like I said, I was the one in charge of the finances. And I would have known anything that he would've said as far as the finances goes.

Back to the reason why I feel that it is important to tell the truth now, like I said, I could have told the truth before, but I was afraid. **I felt that I was pressured to just go ahead with the story.** I was being reminded how I was doing the right thing, that this is a good thing that I'm doing. I was doing the right thing and as well, I did have to remind myself that I could be incriminated. So, I felt that, 'okay, if you tell me a hundred times that it's the right thing to do, if that's what all of the agents are telling me, then it is the right thing to do.' I didn't feel that it was the right thing to do, but I was being told it was the right thing to do. **I felt really, really pressured.** I know you can say that why don't I feel pressured now; It's not that I don't feel pressured now, I just feel that the truth has to come out. There's no way that any person in their right mind can go ahead and live the rest of their life knowing that they sent somebody to jail for life on lies. There is no way. And there is no way I can live the rest of my life knowing that Malachi is going to spend the rest of his life in jail, knowing that Kathy is in jail now because of charges that we brought up against her. Every time I look at my children, I think about her children. I think about the fact that her children doesn't have her and it's not right, it's just not right.

I'm also going to talk about the money situation. Yes, I was in charge of the finances, and a lot of the financial decisions that were made, were by me, at the time that I was in charge. When I wasn't in charge, when it was Kathy that was in charge, the financial decisions were made by her. **Malachi did not make financial decisions.** *We collected the money, we separated the money. When I was in charge, I was in charge of where the money went, how the money was handled, how it was separated.* **He [Dr. Malachi Z. York] never sat us down and told us to avoid the FBI or avoid the IRS or do anything illegal with his money. As a matter of fact, he was very, very serious about handling his finances in a legal way.** *So anything that happened with the finances when I was in charge, it was my decision to decide what happened with the finances, where it went and how it was handled. And the same goes for anybody else who was in charge prior to me or after me. That's how it was done.*

I didn't really understand the structure charges and I believe that I expressed that to the U.S. attorney and I also expressed that to FBI Jalaine [Ward] that I really didn't understand the structure charges and they explained to me that anytime you try to avoid filing that report then that's a serious charge and like I stated previously and I believe I stated this on my testimony on the stand, that Malachi never told us not to file those reports. **He [Dr. Malachi Z. York] never told us to deny any of the tellers any information.** *If we did deposit over $10,000 dollars and if we were investigated, he never told us not to follow through. He never told us not to talk to anyone about it. So that's how I feel about the money structure charges.*

I just want to repeat that the charges brought up against Malachi were all lies. We did back each other's story up. *I can't really speak for why other people did it. I know that a lot of them had their own personal anger issues with Malachi.* **I want to state that nobody that left the community left because they were molested. That was never a reason why anybody left because they were molested or because he was doing things to them that they did not agree to. Nobody left because he was doing any criminal acts. Nobody had any problems with that. That was never the reason for anyone to leave - child or adult. That was never the reason for anybody to leave. Everybody left because they wanted to leave. Because they got fed up. I left because I wanted a new life; it just wasn't for me anymore. Some people did get kicked out**

but it was never because of any child molestation issues. Nobody ever left because they felt that they were molested. There was no child that ever, ever made a statement that "I want to leave because Malachi's molesting me." That never took place. That never happened. *Like I said, the charges were all personal charges, it was all because of personal reasons.*

Jacob had at different points in time, questioned us about "well what about this boy or what about this girl, what do you think he's going to say? What do you think she's going to say? Did you ever see anything happen with this girl? And I would always tell Jacob "I've never seen anything happen with this boy or girl" but Jacob forced us, he really, really wanted us to say, 'okay this happened with this boy, this happened with this girl,' "well if you are going to say it then you might as well tell them." So he questioned all of us about different people, and like I said, everybody had their own personal reasons, everybody had their reason for feeling that they had to tell the story. *For me, it was because I was in charge, and I felt pressured, I felt compelled that anything that anybody told the FBI about me, it would be so hard for me to try to prove that it was a lie or prove that it was not the truth and like I said, I was never represented by my own personal attorney, I didn't really know my rights, I don't really understand the law. I wasn't really told or I would say I was not really informed about everything that was going on. I know there was charges brought up against Malachi, I knew that we had to testify. I knew what we had to say. That was it,* I did not understand that I could just get another attorney and speak to another attorney about not going through. There was so many times where I wanted to pull back my statement, when I wanted to just not go through with it but I didn't have the support, I didn't have the backup, I didn't feel that I had the protection, you know, yes I was afraid of going to jail, I was afraid of having my children taken away from me, I know that it's not right to be afraid for myself and think that it was right "okay, I can protect myself and he still go to jail" I know that that is not right. I know that it was a selfish thought and that's why I'm here now, to tell the truth, to tell how it was.

In conclusion, it's really, really time for the truth to come out. This is going on two years or, I think it actually has been **two years [18 years now in 2020 A.D.]** *So many people have suffered. Malachi's suffering day by day because of this, and it's really, really not fair.* **I really, really believe that somebody had to come out with the truth** *and like I said, every day I think about him suffering. Every day, I think about how wrong it is.* **What we've all done, how wrong it is. Every day I think about what happened to all of the lives of those children. So this is why I'm putting my statement on record because it's the right thing to do. And like I said, I want the truth to come out, I can't be afraid anymore. I can't feel pressured anymore. I can't say that, you know, I can't go on with the rest of my life knowing that I'm hiding the truth, I'm holding the truth. I think it's time for it to come out. It has to come out, you know, we have to bring out the truth behind all these lies that was put out. We have to do the right thing. And I'm here because I want to do the right thing. Because I really want to do the right thing. That's it."**

[END OF Habibah "Abigail" Washington's Recant Video dated April 18, 2004 A.D.]

Narrator - *"Detectives interview this former cult member for several hours. She then provides the names of more women that want to come forward."*

Fact - Why did "People Magazine" not give you the name of "this former cult member" who was present and testified as the Government's key witness during Dr. York's 2004 A.D. Trial but provide the name of Jacob York who wasn't present at Dr. York's 2004 A.D. Trial? The reason being is because "this former cult member" is Habiybah Washington and in Habiybah Washington's Recant video she exposes the Conspiracy and lies against Dr. Malachi Z. York. The full video is STILL available to the public via

YouTube. Don't believe me, Check it out! What Jacob York and the conspirators didn't realize is that the cup they wanted for Dr. York; They will have to drink it.

Jess Cagle - *"Niki faces a lot of pressure to stay, both from York and from her own mother, who's not interested in leaving the cult."*

Fact - The reason why "Niki faces a lot of pressure to stay" is because while in the Community everything was provided and you didn't have to go OUTSIDE to get a JOB. Of course Niki's mother is not interested in leaving a community where everything was provided for her. This is confirmed in Niki's testimony during Dr. York's 2004 A.D. Trial and I quote **Niki's Direct Examination by Ms. Thacker:**

Ms. Thacker - *"When you said you were told to get a regular job, what does that mean?"*
Niki (Nicole Lopez) - *"Before then, everybody basically worked on the land... But for the most part, nobody on the land had regular, you know, 9:00 to 5:00 jobs where they would go outside, get a job, get a paycheck."*
   [January 12, 2004 A.D. Trial Testimony Case 5:02-CR-27-CAR]

Jess Cagle - *"Now York is not happy with Niki's decision to leave. So to save face he announces that he's kicking Niki out and he arranges a car to drive her to Atlanta."*

Fact - Dr. Malachi Z. York is not the type of person to "save face." That's not Dr. Malachi Z. York's character. Dr. York is a "savior" but not one to "save face." Dr. Malachi Z. York is continuously scorned and mocked for who and what he is - THE Master Teacher. Dr. York has been slandered, persecuted and has heard all forms of false stories about himself since 1970 A.D. to Now. Dr. York has never been concerned with "Saving face." Dr. York is about his Heavenly Father's business and welcomes the slander because of the many messengers of The Most High who all went through the same trials and tribulations.

Niki (Nicole Lopez) - *"The day I left I was scared and numb and felt like this is it. If I were gonna die then at least I made that one thing. That choice of my own because I didn't have any choices. I had to do what I was told the whole time."*

Fact - This sounds exactly like Cain's sentiments when he was kicked out and left the Garden. (Refer to Genesis 4:13-16) "I didn't have any choices. I had to do what I was told the whole time." This is false. You had a choice and according to your **LETTER NO. 1 FROM NIKI (NICOLE LOPEZ)** you chose to leave and live the lifestyle you inscribed below and I quote:

"<u>I [Niki] definitely miss Kuwsh [minor who Niki was having sex with]. I wish I had the balls enough and left. Instead of being here pretending. I want to experience things, life, no worries, going places, smoking (and not cigarettes) getting drunk without guilt or stealing,</u>"

Remember according to Habiybah's Recant Video "<u>Nicole Lopez [Niki] had a lot of disgruntled issues with Jacob's dad, because for one, she was kicked out and she felt that it was wrong that she was kicked out because she didn't have anywhere to go. She didn't know anybody and after all the years that she lived in the community, Malachi kicked her out, and she had nowhere to go. So she was kind of mad about that.</u>"

Tracy Bowen Deputy Sheriff Putnam County - *"Niki was a very important part of our investigation. This was a way of her saying you know, we're gonna help make this right. I can't take back what happened to them but maybe I can help stop it from happening to other children."*

Fact - Yes Niki was a very important part of the case. Niki had an immunity agreement to protect her from being a child molester and being that Niki did not want to be prosecuted for her crimes and being fueled by her anger for being kicked out; The Feds could use her to say anything they wanted to fabricate a case against Dr. Malachi Z. York. Tracy Bowen is taking advantage of the Public's ignorance of the Facts in the case against Dr. Malachi Z. York. To give you another peek into Dr. York's Trial; Here is the **PROSECUTIONS WITNESS** Issa Johnson's trial testimony for the U.S. Government on Direct examination by U.S. Attorney Richard Moultrie. I repeat, The **PROSECUTIONS WITNESS** and **NOT** the **DEFENSE** for Dr. York. Following the Prosecutions direct examination is The Defense Attorney Adrian Patrick's Cross examination below.

DIRECT EXAMINATION BY PROSECUTING ATTORNEY MR. MOULTRIE BELOW:
Richard Moultrie - *"Did Mr. York ever sexually molest you?"*
Issa Johnson - *"No, Not at all."*
Richard Moultrie - *"Do you know a lady named Janna Waddell?"*
Issa Johnson - *"Yes, I do."*
Richard Moultrie - *"Who is she?"*
Issa Johnson - *"A caseworker."*
Richard Moultrie - *"Is she your caseworker?"*
Issa Johnson - *"Yes."*
Richard Moultrie - *"And do you recall telling Janna Waddell that Mr. York began messing with you when you were 7 or 8?"*
Issa Johnson - *"No."*
Richard Moultrie - *"And that it lasted for about 3 years?"*
Issa Johnson - *"No."*
Richard Moultrie - *"Did you tell Beluwra that Mr. York molested you?"*
Issa Johnson - *"No."*
Richard Moultrie - *"Did you tell Safa'a LaRoche that Mr. York molested you?"*
Issa Johnson - *"No."*

CROSS EXAMINATION BY DEFENSE ATTORNEY MR. PATRICK BELOW:

Adrian Patrick - *"Mr. Johnson, do you recall the day that land was raided?"*

Issa Johnson - *"Yes."*

Adrian Patrick - *"On that day, you were taken into DFCS custody; is that correct?"*

Issa Johnson - *"Yes."*

Adrian Patrick - *"You along with several other children that were on the land, were taken away; correct?"*

Issa Johnson - *"Yes."*

Adrian Patrick - *"On that day were you asked whether or not the defendant had ever molested you?"*

Issa Johnson - *"Was I asked?"*

Adrian Patrick - *"Did anyone ask you that?"*

Issa Johnson - *"Yes."*

Adrian Patrick - *"And what did you tell them?"*

Issa Johnson - *"No."*

Adrian Patrick - *"How many times would you say you were asked on that day?"*

Issa Johnson - *"It was repeatedly, about four times, I guess."*

Adrian Patrick - *"How many times would you say you've been asked whether or not the defendant (Dr. York) has ever molested you since the beginning of this case?"*

Issa Johnson - *"Well, most of the time, they didn't ask me; they told me. Well, she didn't—- basically, yeah she said, "We know this happened to you." She was the one that told me."*

Adrian Patrick - *"Now did you ever tell her (Janna Waddell - caseworker) that you had been messed with, or whatever, messed with, molested by the defendant?"*

Issa Johnson - *"No."*

Adrian Patrick - *"Now, Safa'a LaRoche And Krystal Harden, did you ever tell Safa'a LaRoche that you had been molested by the defendant?"*

Issa Johnson - *"No."*

Adrian Patrick - *"What about Krystal Harden?"*

Issa Johnson - *"No."*
Adrian Patrick - *"Now did Safa'a LaRoche and/or Krystal Harden ever try to get you to say the defendant molested you?"*
Issa Johnson - *"Not Safa'a, But Krystal."*
Adrian Patrick - *"What do you mean? Tell me about that."*
Issa Johnson - *"She was just saying that I should, you know say something happened, <u>and that they can't wait until they get their money</u>, and that I know this is true, things of that sort."*
Adrian Patrick - *"<u>So she was talking about getting money?</u>"*
Issa Johnson - *"<u>Yeah.</u>"*
Adrian Patrick - *"So I'm asking you to tell the truth; Have you ever been molested by the defendant?"*
Issa Johnson - *"No."*
Adrian Patrick - *"Have you ever seen any of the other alleged victims? Have you ever seen any boys being molested by the defendant?"*
Issa Johnson - *"Not at all."*
Adrian Patrick - *"Have you ever seen any girls being molested by the defendant?"*
Issa Johnson - *"No."*
Adrian Patrick - *"You remained in the organization from 1988 until I guess 2002?"*
Issa Johnson - *"Yes."*
Adrian Patrick - *"During that entire period of time, have you ever seen Amanda Noel being molested?"*
Issa Johnson - *"No."*
Adrian Patrick - *"David Noel?"*
Issa Johnson - *"No"*
Adrian Patrick - *"Muniyra Franklin?"*
Issa Johnson - *"No, I have not."*
[January 12, 2004 A.D. Trial Testimony Case 5:02-CR-27-CAR]

Christine Pelisek - *"The law enforcement in Georgia didn't want to have a repeat of Waco [David Koresh & The Branch Davidians]. So there was a lot of concern about how they were gonna deal with Dwight York."*

Fact - Robbie Ward - Administrator/Researcher who was on the land gives her account of the day Law Enforcement invaded the land on May 8, 2002 A.D. in the Documentary entitled **Mysteries Behind Closed Doors: The Untold Truth of the Dr. Malachi Z. York Case (2010 A.D.)** where she says the following and I quote: *"You hear a bang at the door [office] and a big explosion type sound at the basement, they blew out the window... glass shattered and women just screaming. They're [armed guards] like 'LAY DOWN, LAY DOWN' We're all laying down on the floor, one of the sisters she has an asthma attack. Man comes up the steps and points the gun directly in her face... They came to kill. They brought in over 200 agents. They flew them in from California, Washington D.C., Atlanta. They made this a big effort but what a lot of people don't know was, the raid was planned for 3am in the morning while everybody was asleep.* **By the grace of The Most High it didn't happen at that time** *because it definitely would have been a slaughter and bloodbath. And on the news it might have been chalked up as 'Oh they killed themselves or It was a war, men women and children had guns.'* **They literally came with the Freezer Trucks and body bags because that is what they had expected and what they had planned for.**" *I'm glad that Doc [Dr. York] wasn't here because the reality is that's who they wanted to kill...That's my personal feelings for that on a raid that you plan for 3am in the morning"*

Law enforcement the day of the invasion went to Dr. York's place of residence in Athens, Georgia. Dr. York was not living in the community in Eatonton, Georgia and had not been living in Eatonton on the land for some years. Thomas Chism who was at Dr. York's residence at 155 Mansfield Court in Athens, Georgia gives his account when law enforcement came to the property the day of in the **Winner for the Best Social Justice Documentary New York International Film & Video Festival 2010 Documentary** entitled **"Mysteries Behind Closed Doors: The Untold Truth of the Dr. Malachi Z. York Case" (2010 A.D.)** and I quote: *"So I looked out there and I see all these men in black, Police officers in black and* *they were running trying to circle the house. So I said 'alright they're gonna bust-in to myself.' So I went to the front door and opened it and they were getting ready to bust the door down. When they saw me, they all stopped and looked at me in surprise because they didn't get a chance to break the door down. They came in bum-rushed me, threw me on the ground, hand-cuffed me. I told them look 'there's a woman upstairs, she got two kids, don't hurt them [pleadingly]...So they run upstairs and during that time the sister heard the commotion and she took her babies and hid in the closet and when* **they [officers] came up-stairs, broke open the door and pointed the guns at her little two-year-old-child."**

Ziyaad Muhammad LaRoche - Art Designer/Painter who was also on the land gives his account of the day Law Enforcement invaded the land on May 8, 2002 A.D. in the Documentary entitled **Mysteries Behind Closed Doors: The Untold Truth of the Dr. Malachi Z. York Case (2010 A.D.)** where he says the following and I quote: *"Guys [Law Enforcement] jumped out, 'Don't move, freeze, Don't move, FBI,' I put my hands up and all I had in my hands was a paint brush, literally one paint brush in my hands...Two guys come and frisk me, they take everything out of my pockets and they snatch me up, pick me up off the ground and took me to the other side toward where the barn was and just dropped me on the ground and I could feel a gun to the back of my head, felt like a shotgun or something that could kill me basically...I was like what's going on? [Officers] Shut up, Don't fu@#!%& say nothing!"*

So, if Law Enforcement didn't want a repeat of Waco; Why was the "Raid" planned for 3am in the morning?!

Jalaine Ward (retired FBI Agent) - *"We learn from radio communications that his vehicle had pulled into a parking lot of a grocery store. The S.W.A.T. Team was there and the arrest teams. Our Job was to make sure we could Identify him. He got out of the vehicle with the female and was going in the grocery store. It was at that point we see the arrest go down."*

Fact - On May 8, 2002 A.D. Dr. Malachi Z. York was arrested in a parking lot of a K-Mart shopping center in Milledgeville, Georgia by FBI and over 100 law enforcement officers. At the time Dr. York was held by the Federal District of Middle Georgia on 4 counts of Transporting in interstate commerce or causing to be transported in interstate commerce children under the age of 16 for the purpose of engaging in criminal sexual activity in violation of Title 18 USC Section 2423 (a) as well as traveling in interstate commerce for the purpose of engaging in a sexual act with a juvenile in violation of Title 18 USC Section 2423 (b). Dr. York's wife Kathy Johnson was charged with one count of Transporting and causing to be transported children under the age of 16 in interstate commerce for the purpose of engaging in criminal sexual activity in violation of title 18 USC 2423 (a). Dr. York and Kathy were being represented by Attorney (Senator) Leroy Johnson - the first African American to serve in the legislature since 1907 A.D. Before The Honorable Claude Hicks - U.S. Magistrate Judge on May 9, 2002 A.D.; Attorney Leroy Johnson informed the Court that his clients would be entering a **plea of not guilty** to all counts. On May 13, 2002 A.D. the Motion seeking the pretrial detention of Dr. York and Kathy Johnson was heard before the court.

New Attorney for the Defense Ed Garland on May 13, 2002 A.D. noticed something abnormal to which he stated, _"I understand there's a parallel child molestation case in the state, and this is very unusual. I would venture there are 5 thousand or 4 thousand a year with no federal jurisdiction assumed. So there's something we don't know obviously going on here of some significance, significant enough that the Federal Government has chosen to make a federal charge out of a state child molestation claim._ **There may be factors relating to the parents of the alleged victim that go to bias, motive, to frame these--for false charge."**

Now let's take a look at the character of Jalaine Ward who appeared On the July 9, 2018 A.D. **(Investigation Discovery)** I.D. Channel broadcast episode 6 People Magazine Investigates Cults:

On May 13, 2002 A.D. via Direct Examination by U.S. Attorney for the Government Richard Moultrie; **Agent Jalaine G. Ward of the Federal Bureau of Investigation** testified under oath that Dr. York had a 1964 misdemeanor rape conviction and that, "he (Dr.York) was 18 at the time that he had sex with a 13 year old." However according to the Report by The US PROBATION OFFICE NO. 7773 pg. 29 it shows that Dr. York was 18 and his girlfriend was 16 **NOT** 13. This was misinformation by an FBI agent under oath for the sole purpose of demonizing Dr. York to show an alleged pattern of behavior that never existed with Dr. York. **FBI Agent Jalaine Ward** on May 14, 2002 A.D. said, "They (Law Enforcement) found photographs of children in sexually explicitly positions and other items of evidence.... several eight millimeter tapes etcetera." Ed Garland for the Defense asked Agent Jalaine Ward "Was Mr. York in the Photographs?" Agent Jalaine Ward replied, "I believe he is in some--I don't know that yet without looking at them myself." This belief of FBI Agent Jalaine Ward can be weighed with her other beliefs about Dr. York to ascertain the truth. Defense Attorney Ed Garland asked FBI Agent Jalaine Ward, "Did you find these passports you told about when you were out there (Tama-Re)? FBI Agent Jalaine Ward replied, "I am told that we found numerous passports and membership application. I have not seen them myself yet." Ed Garland then replies, "...are you familiar with the fact that in the passport under "important information" it states This is a novelty passport, it's only valid for the Holy Land (Tama-Re), it is not legally intended to be used for traveling to other countries... Were you familiar with that fact? Agent Jalaine Ward replies, "I have not had a chance to review the passports." Ed Garland: Nobody during your investigation told you these were novelty passports like you get at Disney World? FBI Agent Jalaine Ward: No, sir.

FBI Agent Jalaine Ward believed Dr. York had sex with a 13 year old while 18 years old which was false (one Incident). FBI Agent Jalaine Ward believed Dr. York was in photos in sexually explicit positions and said "I don't know that yet without looking at them myself" (co-Incidents or two Incidents). FBI Agent Jalaine Ward mistakenly believed "Novelty Passports" for legal passports due to a *lack of due diligence in an attempt to implicate a pattern of behavior with Dr. York that doesn't exist. Yet, a pattern of misinformation and lack of research is revealed by FBI Agent Jalaine Ward. (three Incidents is a REALITY).*

This case as of May 14, 2002 A.D. against Dr. York was based on traveling and transporting for the purpose of having sex with a minor. **Defense Attorney Ed Garland asked the FBI Agent Jalaine Ward in regards to this case:** *"Now in connection with the travel for the purpose of having sex with a minor, do you have a witness who says that the purpose in the travel was to have the children have sex?" FBI Agent Jalaine Ward replied,* **"No, not that says that, no."**

Nowhere in the entire so-called Documentary did People Magazine use Jalaine Ward's May 13, 2002 A.D. testimony stating that Dr. York had sex with a 13 year old while he was 18. Wouldn't that have been fitting to support their position of Dr. York being this Monster they are trying to portray? The reason it was not used is because it was not true. The truth is catching up to their lies and they know this.

On May 14, 2002 A.D. **Magistrate Judge Claude Hicks** at the **Detention Hearing** stated and I quote, *"I think to a great extent that's what's been presented to me in the courtroom today, and it's not unlike the situation which I imagined existed in courtrooms earlier in previous years with individuals like Jimmy Swaggart, Jim Jones, Jim Baker. They had a quite a few loyal followers. They let their followers down. That may ultimately be what the outcome of this case is. It may not be. That's not for me to say."*

[May 14, 2002 A.D. Detention Hearing Case 5:02-CR-27-(HL)]

Judge Hicks compared Dr. York to Jimmy Swaggart - involved in sex scandals with prostitutes; Jim Jones - hailed as the infamous mass suicide cult leader and Jim Bakker - renowned televangelist imprisoned for fraud and conspiracy. The U.S. Magistrate Judge Claude Hicks contributed to the destruction of Dr. York's presumption of innocence during the May 14, 2002 A.D. Hearing. Presumption of Innocence means when one is accused of a crime they are innocent until proven guilty. An accusation doesn't prove guilt. However, your right to be viewed as innocent can be destroyed by negative influences of the media, slander and libel etc. When the media or Court makes negative statements about you before or during a court proceeding, that creates a false sense of guilt that potential jurors and the public will take for granted and thus see the accused as guilty until proven innocent which interferes with their right to a fair and impartial process.

As soon as Judge Claude Hicks destroyed Dr. York's presumption of Innocence he gives the false impression that Dr. York & Kathy Johnson had it by saying, *"the presumption of innocence will be with these defendants as they go to trial"* etc. The presumption of Innocence was never with Dr. York because the media in the middle district of Georgia had over 5 years of negative news publicity about Dr. York and Nuwaubians before Dr. York's arrest May 8, 2002 A.D.

Narrator - *"York pleads guilty in state court to 74 counts of child molestation. Then he pleads guilty in Federal Court to the transportation of minors for criminal sexual activity, conspiracy and racketeering."*

Fact - Dr. Malachi Z. York did not plead guilty. This is misinformation that has been fed to the public since January 23, 2003 A.D. when Dr. Malachi Z. York was FORCED to sign a plea agreement under duress in Federal Court and January 24, 2003 A.D. in State Court and I quote the **June 30, 2003 A.D. Hearing Before United States District Judge Hugh Lawson:**

Judge Hugh Lawson - *"Let me ask you this. I'm trying to understand about your plea in January."*
Dr. Malachi Z. York - *"Right. I was under duress."*
Judge Hugh Lawson - *"Was that an involuntary -- did you want to with enter that plea?"*
Dr. Malachi Z. York - *"I was under duress."*

Judge Hugh Lawson - *"Well, does that mean that it was invalid plea?"*
Dr. Malachi Z. York - *"No, it means that I was under duress..... after being tortured and given inhumane treatment and mental persuasion by officers of the court telling me that "if you don't do this, you're going to get a thousand years, "I don't think we would win this case, and then once I went before the Court of Putnam County and I saw the circle of three and how they worked together -- the Judge, the Sheriff, the D.A., and they was denying every one of our motions, regardless of what it was; like today, another motion, just bang -- they made it look like, sir [Judge], it was no way possible a human being was going to get a fair trial in this court.* They made it look like a racial issue to me. "Listen, you're basically a black man and you're not going to get a fair trial in here." So we asked for a venue move, sir. And instead of them moving it to a suitable environment, they moved it to, let's say, 20 miles away. Anybody who goes to K-Mart and can't find a product in K-Mart, the next step is to go to Covington, so everybody in Covington already knew the case before I got there. *So I was on the cross already, sir. The crucifixion was there. The nails were going in. And all I was asking for is a fair trial; that's all. I think I'm entitled to a fair trial, but in my court."*
Judge Hugh Lawson - *"...Now, you said that the plea that you entered in January was under duress?*
Dr. Malachi Z. York - *"Yes, sir. I felt I was under duress.*
Judge Hugh Lawson - *"It was forced?"*
Dr. Malachi Z. York - *"No, I was under duress. I don't want to add words."*

This is called a *False Guilty Plea*. A False Guilty Plea is when you accept a Plea offer from the prosecutor for a crime that you did NOT commit. It is when an innocent man or woman is forced to plead guilty by threats, intimidation and fear tactics. Dr. Malachi Z. York plead guilty on the pretense that his plea would deliver his co- defendants - Kathy Johnson, Khadijah Merrit, Chandra Lampkin and Istiyr Cole from their incarceration. Dr. York was sleeping on a concrete floor, not receiving medication for his life threatening illness - Acute Hereditary Angioedema which can cause sudden death, deprived of visits from his personal physician, in a rat-and-roach infested cell, sleep deprived and starving. Dr. York was told by attorney Ed Garland (whom Dr. York never hired) that his co- defendants (mothers with children) were being treated under the same harsh conditions. Also to mention, Kathy Johnson was suffering from M.S. and without her medication it would be crippling. Ed Garland lied to Dr. York about the state of affairs of Dr. York's co-defendants because by the time Dr. York signed the plea agreement on January 23 & 24 2003 A.D.; Kathy Johnson, Khadijah Merrit, Chandra Lampkin and Istiyr Cole had already been released almost 2 months. Dr. York was not given the facts by Ed Garland. Dr. York did not receive any communication from the Garland firm. Dr. York's so-called attorney Ed Garland coerced Dr. York to make the false guilty plea under the pretense that Dr. York's co-defendants were still incarcerated. What Dr. York did is what Dr. York always does and that is sacrifice himself for others. Jesus said it best in **John 15:13** *"Greater love hath no man than this, that a man lay down his life for his friends."* Dr. York expressed the fact that he did not receive any lawyer visits which was not contested and I quote:

Judge Hugh Lawson - *"Do you understand what we're doing here today?"*
Dr. Malachi Z. York - *"Yes, I do. I vaguely understand what the process that's going on, I am -- totally upset by the fact that I wasn't informed. I never got any documents, no lawyer visits."*
Judge Hugh Lawson - *"What were you not informed about?"*
Dr. Malachi Z. York - <u>*"I wasn't even -- I wasn't informed about this case or when I was coming to court. I didn't know about the May 29th case. I was not informed. Nobody came to see me. I didn't get no documents."*</u>

[June 30, 2003 A.D. Hearing Before United States District Judge Hugh Lawson]

Jess Cagle - *"Now he's expected to receive a 15 year sentence for his plea bargain but the Judge ultimately rejects that and sends the case to trial."*

Fact - Judge Hugh Lawson on June 30, 2003 A.D. rejected the January 23, 2003 A.D. "plea agreement" because he said and I quote: *"...The Court finds that the stipulated sentence does not adequately address the severity of the admitted and alleged criminal conduct of the defendant...the plea agreement is rejected for those reasons."* **[Refer to the June 30, 2003 A.D. Hearing Before United States District Judge Hugh Lawson]** However, Jess Cagle leaves out the fact that Judge Hugh Lawson was disqualified aka recused because of his rejection to which newly assigned Judge Charles Ashley Royal became the Trial Judge.

Ed Garland - *"As to the position, the actual position of the pleadings and the issues is that Mr. York has been afforded the opportunity before* **Judge Hugh Lawson disqualified himself to withdraw his previously tendered plea**, *and he has not yet withdrawn that plea."*
    [August 6, 2003 A.D. Hearing Before United States District Judge C. Ashley Royal]

Notice the subtle removal of critical information that "People Magazine" leaves out to give a fraudulent depiction of what really took place. Jess Cagle makes it appear that the same Judge who rejected the plea was the Judge who presided over the Trial and that's not true like so many other things that "People" believe about Dr. Malachi Z. York.

Christine Pelisek - *"York absolutely did not want to go to trial because all his secrets would come out and all the sexual deviance over the last, you know, decade or so would come out and that is the last thing he wanted."*

Fact - This is absolutely false and the last statement of the documentary that warrants a very necessary rebuttal. You will shortly be provided with the **Final Argument By Mr. Patrick on behalf of Dr. Malachi Z. York** that the public did not get a chance to hear or see and the real reason why Dr. Malachi Z. York's 2004 A.D. trial was sealed from the Public. After Dr. Malachi Z. York's 2004 A.D. Trial (January 5th - January 23rd); Dr. York did a series of recorded telephone conversations in the Month of March 2004 A.D. from Jones County Jail in Gray, Georgia entitled **"Maku Speaks from the Isles of Patmos"** where Dr. York answered questions concerning the case against him and any concerns that his loved ones might have where he said and I quote: **"I want the public to demand to want to see every detail of this case and monitor every detail so they can see that it's a lie."** Another strange thing about this documentary is that nowhere in the entire broadcast did **"People Magazine"** mention the "structuring cash transactions to evade currency reporting requirements" charge against Dr. York that was mentioned in The Court's Narrative by Judge Charles Ashley Royal on January 5, 2004 A.D. - The first day of Dr. Malachi Z. York's Trial. Neil Dukoff of The Dukoff and Company Certified Public Accountants Firm testified on Dr. Malachi Z. York's behalf during the 2004 A.D. Trial. Dr. York was a client of the The Dukoff and Company firm for 30 years from father to son. Neil Dukoff's testimony was to dispute the money structure charges. Below is Neil Dukoff's trial testimony by Attorney Cedric Davis.

Cedric Davis - *"How long have you been providing accounting services for Mr. York?"*
Neil Dukoff - *"Well, our firm has been providing accounting and tax services to Mr. York for about 30 years."*
Cedric Davis - *"Okay, And you personally, how long have you been doing or providing tax services or accounting services for Mr. York?"*
Neil Dukoff - *"I've been indirectly or directly involved in his returns for about 15 years."*
Cedric Davis - *"And for the relevant period of time, do you have some tax returns with you today?"*
Neil Dukoff - *"Yes, I do."*

Cedric Davis - *"And what years do you have?"*
Neil Dukoff - *"I have 1996 through 2001."*
Cedric Davis - *"Can you tell us what those documents represent?"*
Neil Dukoff - *"They're the Federal Income Tax filings for Malachi York for the years that we just—1996 to 2001."*
Cedric Davis - *"The exhibits that we have identified, are those documents that you prepared for Mr. York?"*
Neil Dukoff - *"Oh, yes."*
Cedric Davis - *"Do you have any knowledge whether or not those documents were actually filed with the IRS?"*
Neil Dukoff - *"Yes."*
Cedric Davis - *"During the time that you have or your firm has assisted Mr. York in his accounting business, has he ever been audited by the government?"*
Neil Dukoff - *"No."*
Cedric Davis - *"And I ask you again, are you aware of anything that requires you—that makes it illegal to keep cash in your home?"*
Neil Dukoff - *"No."*
Cedric Davis - *"In all the years that you prepared Mr. York's tax return, you've always filed his taxes as Malachi York?"*
Neil Dukoff - *"Yes, based on what I have here, sure."*
Cedric Davis - *"Have you ever known him as Dwight York?"*
Neil Dukoff - *"I personally haven't, no."*
Cedric Davis - *"Has the IRS ever had any problem with the way it's been filled?"*
Neil Dukoff - *"No."*
Cedric Davis - *"Or contacted you in any kind of way?"*
Neil Dukoff - *"Never got any correspondence on it."*
Cedric Davis - *"Mr. Dukoff, because individuals deposit less than $10,000 in the bank, does that equate to money structuring in your opinion?"*
Neil Dukoff - *"No."*

[January 12, 2004 A.D. Trial Testimony Case 5:02-CR-27-CAR]

Final Argument by Adrian Patrick - The Lead Trial Attorney for Dr. Malachi Z. York

Mr. Patrick - *"Thank you, Your Honor. Good Morning, ladies and gentleman."*

ALL - *"Good Morning."*

Mr. Patrick - *"I'd like to thank you all for the opportunity to present this case to you. I asked you to do one thing in the beginning, and this is a very long complex case, and I asked you to listen to the complete case, and you did that. You continually took notes, and we noticed that. And my client [Dr. York] and myself, we thank you for doing that, because it's an extremely long case, three and a-half weeks, and you're talking about emotional type of issues. With the case of child molestation, it's human nature to just believe that it's true. It's just human nature, because nobody likes child molestation. Nobody likes that. So, with that being human nature to believe that it's true, <u>you tend to kind of forget that it could possibly not be true.</u> And because of that, you never ask yourself the question <u>"What if these allegations are not true?</u> What if the entire group of people that are* saying it never happened -- What if they're telling the truth? What if the other people that are saying it happened are not telling the truth? But because of the type of charges, human nature causes you to think that child molestation, whatever the allegation, is true. But I want you to ask yourself the question, "What if Malachi York is not guilty? What if all of these individuals that got on the stand during our case that said nothing happened, What if they are telling the truth? Now I want to point out something to you. The defense has absolutely no obligation to present any evidence at all. It's the government's burden to prove their case beyond a reasonable doubt. And I ask this question: When the government rested, did they prove their case beyond a reasonable doubt to you? Did they present all the witnesses that were in the indictment so you can hear from those witnesses as to whether or not these allegations were true? Or, were they depending on you to say, "Oh, we have several acts of child molestation?" They were depending on you to do as they did and do what human nature calls you to do and say. "Because it's child molestation, he must be guilty." I would ask you to put up the first exhibit. Why didn't the government present these alleged victims? What were they trying to hide? Suhaila Williams, she's in the indictment as an alleged victim in this case. Sakinah Woods, she's in the indictment as an alleged victim. We put her up in our case. This is unprecedented; a defendant has to put up an alleged victim in his case to explain this never happened. Why didn't the government in their case put up Suhaila Thomas? Suhaila Thomas is an alleged victim in this case. The government attacked Suhaila Thomas, but they put her in the indictment. And if the government truly believed that Suhaila Thomas said that the defendant molested her, why didn't they present her in their case to you? They rested and did not present her. Hanaan Merrit, she's an alleged victim. They did not present her. Qiturah Lampkin, she's an alleged victim. They never even talked to her. She was never spoken to. The first time she came to any type of court is when I called her to the stand to speak to you. She never spoke to any Law Enforcement Officer. No Law Enforcement Officer went to her and said, "Are these allegations true?" They didn't even talk to her at all. That's an indication that the government is depending on you to just say, "Because it's child molestation, he must be guilty." Why didn't they present Ebony Henry? We presented Ebony Henry to indicate that nothing ever happened. Rodeya Herbert; Why didn't the government present Rodeya Herbert to you? She's in the indictment. Hasnaa Evans; why didn't they present her in their case? Husna Evans, why didn't they present her in their case?

These are 10 alleged victims that are in the indictment in the defense's case and we don't have to present any witnesses. We presented these individuals so that you could get a complete story, a complete idea of the the true nature of this case. What were they trying to hide? The reason that the government did not present these 10 alleged victims is because it would cause you to do something that is against human nature. It would cause you to ask the question, "Maybe he's not guilty." Now I want to present to you some objective evidence in support of why Malachi York is not guilty. These are objective things, because what you have in this case is you have a group of people saying that it didn't happen, "I didn't see it happen to those other people," and you have a group of people saying it did happen, "And I saw it happen with these people." Now, let's talk about some objective things to get beyond the "he say/she say" things. Okay? Now, one, there's absolutely no alleged victims that identify any type marks on Malachi York's body. No tattoos, no scars, marks, nothing. Nothing was mentioned. Two, there's minimal to no description of severe pain associated with this alleged anal assault, vaginal penetration; very little. You're talking about Amanda Noel who allegedly was 9 years old when a 40-year-old man anally raped her and she says it was just a little blood. That's it. Now, I understand that the Doctors got on the stand and said that, "Well, you know, anal injuries heal," and things like that. But I'm asking for your common sensibilities here. All of these children allegedly were raped aggressively by a 40-year-old man, and there's little to no description of severe pain or bleeding or anything. Three, there's absolutely no talk of, "I have bloody underwear, bloody panties," nothing at all. Number four, there's absolutely no video-taped or audio-taped statements of any of the alleged victim's statements that Malachi York molested them, absolutely none. The officers just decided not to take video-tape or audio-tape statements so that you could make a fair assessment when you have one person saying, "I didn't tell the officers this" and the officers saying, "Well, they did." Number five, there's an absolute and complete absence of any allegation of child molestation from the organization's beginning in 1973 to 1988. In the beginning of the case, we presented -- I presented to you several older members of the organization that had been in the organization since 1973, '74, '77. There's absolutely no allegations whatsoever for that entire -- period... There's absolutely no videos or DVDs of Malachi York molesting children. Nothing - The government presented you nothing related to that. There's absolutely no pictures of Malachi York molesting children. There's absolutely no nude pictures of Mr. York with or without anyone. There's absolutely no child pornography. There's absolutely no nude pictures found of any of the alleged victims. Out of over 500 DVDs and videos, only 18 were pornographic. That is less than four percent of the total. Abigail Washington used an alias, Gail Washington, to order and receive her DVDs, and she admitted she did this while she was in the organization; Gail Washington, P.O. Box 6760. Also, if Malachi York used the Pink Panther and the baby oil, why didn't he take it with him when he moved to Athens? Why was it still in Eatonton in the main house when the last person to live there was Abigail Washington? Abigail Washington's father indicated to you that she renovated the house, changed the carpet, paint, curtains -- she brought in her little things -- the alcohol, the Pink Panthers, the videos, the pornographic DVD's. She basically knew where everything was when she was talking to the FBI, so they could go right in and say, "Oh, here's the Pink Panther, here's the liquor," but none of these things found in Athens property.

 Now, if Abigail Washington truly thought Malachi York was a child molester, why would she allow her two children to come back, live and visit with Mr. York two weeks prior to the raid while he was living in Athens? Now, Issa Johnson, Hasnaa Evans, Husna Evans, Qiturah Lampkin, Hanaan Meritt, Suhaila Thomas, Sakinah

········ BIOGRAPHICAL REBUTTAL TO PEOPLE MAGAZINE ········

Woods, and Ebony Hill told you in person under oath that they were never molested; they were never solicited, they never solicited anyone for sex for Malachi York; that no-one solicited them for sex; and they never saw any children being molested, including the alleged victims. Thus, seven of the alleged victims saw nothing happen at all. If this amount of sex was occurring on these pillows that they have here, why didn't the government present you any DNA evidence? They alleged the pillows were with Malachi York from New York all the way to the time he got to Eatonton. They presented no DNA evidence whatsoever. And if this amount of sex was occurring, why was there no- one under the age of 16 or 17 pregnant, or under the age of 17 impregnated? The government would have you believe that Malachi York was so skillful, that he was able to have sex this number of times, unprotected sex, and carefully plan out how not to get one girl pregnant or any girl pregnant at all. Now, another thing, the "Nathara" or "Nathada" person, if there's actually a Nathada or Nathara that was actually the one to introduce Abigail Washington and Nicole Lopez to sex, why didn't the government bring her in? They mentioned Rodeya. We know who Rodeya is. We subpoenaed Rodeya to come. If there was a Nathara, why wasn't she here? The presented no picture of her to you. Rodeya didn't know Nathara. Mildred Cosme, who has been a member of the organization since '81, never heard of a Nathara. There's no Nathara. They created that so that they can create someone to make it appear that someone brought them there. Nicole Lopez even changed -- when her report clearly stated to Joan Cronier that Rodeya did all this videotaping and picture-taking, well, when they found out that Rodeya was not going to support this and that we could get Rodeya here to show that she's not telling the truth, all of a sudden, "Oh, it wasn't Rodeya; it's Nathara." Where's Nathara? Now, we found Rodeya, Jessie Hill, and she stated that Nicole Adah Lopez and Abigail Washington are untruthful and no such events took place. They did a lot of surveillance on Malachi York, but there's no surveillance tapes showing Malachi York engaged in any illegal activity. There are no surveillance tapes showing children leaving Malachi York's home. If Malachi York is such a dangerous person, as they try to state, why are there no interests in any of the alleged victims? Everybody came in and testified -- If what we're saying about Jacob York lying and plotting against Malachi York, if that isn't true, why didn't the government bring Jacob York in to tell you that wasn't true? Jacob brought Abigail Washington to the first meeting with the FBI. Jacob York was available. Why didn't they bring him in to refute what we're saying if it wasn't true? If the government truly believed, as I stated before, that Suhaila Thomas really made that statement, why didn't they call her during their case? There's absolutely no conclusive medical evidence to support these widespread allegations. Many of the exams were normal, and most were non-specific and inconclusive. The doctors were even saying normal exams were consistent; abnormal exams were consistent. What exam is it that shows there's no sexual abuse? People, everybody, the government officers, the medical professionals, because there's the allegation of child molestation, they did what human nature does and assumed that it's true, but nobody asked, "What if it isn't true?"

As far as the money structuring, Malachi York reported all income, filed all tax returns, and paid all taxes for 30 years. He was never audited by the IRS. He never had allegations of money structuring until Abigail Washington and Nicole Harden were in the finance office; and after they left, no more allegations; before they came, no allegations of money structuring. The accountant showed you his tax returns. We got them from over '96 to 2001 where he filed taxes, reported gross receipts of over one million dollars, paid taxes every year. Why all of a sudden for a few years, he says, "Well, I don't want to report over $10,000?" He's reporting over one million dollars to the IRS and paying all of his taxes. Tomeika Pittman told you that the only logical explanation she can give for money structuring is he's evading taxes. He didn't evade any taxes. He's not charged with that. He filed his taxes for 30 years. An additional point, Abigail Washington, when asked, "On those specific dates of the money structuring, can you say that there was more money to be deposited." She stated, "No, I would have to go back on those dates and see how much cash there was supposed to be deposited because that may have been all of the money that should have been deposited." She said the IRS agents gave her examples. That's what she stated. So, there's absolutely no proof on those dates in this indictment that there should have been more money deposited than the $10,000. All right. Also, there's another practical point I would like to make. I outlined the number of times that the witnesses alleged sex acts occurred. The question I have for you, "Is it physically possible?" Amanda Noel, we estimated, said that from '93 to about '99 -- well, '93 to '95, about 2 to 3 times per week; '95 to 2001, about 1 to 2 times per week. So, we added all those up and came up with a total of about -- a total of 1,092 times that he had sexual activity allegedly with Amanda Noel. Now, with Nicole Adah Lopez, she stated from '93 to '95, virtually every day; from '95 to 2000, approximately 2 times per week. So, if you go each year and down to your total, it's 1,306 times. Now, Khalid Eddington, or Eddie, he alleged that from '93 to '96, about 3 times per week, a total of 624 times. Well, Salha Eddington, she gave no particular amount of time, so we didn't add that into the total. David Noel, from '93 to '95, he alleged 2 to 3 times per week; '95 to 2001, he alleged 3 to 4 times per week. Go up to the total. That would mean that there were 1,768 times. Salaam Shilamooh LaRoche, he stated it was a total of about 9 times. Jin Hee, Ginger -- I'm not sure how you have it written in your notes -- she stated about 1 time per week from '93 to '95; about 156 times. Abigail Washington, there was no particular frequency given. Atiyah Thomas, from '93 to 2001, total time would have been about 1,404 times. Sakinah Parham alleged from '93 to '99, 3 times per week; total 1,092 times from '93 to '99. Ebony Hill alleged from 1990 to 1997 2 to 3 times per week. The total would have been 1,248 times. Nicole Harden alleged from '93 to 2000 about a total of 4 times. Qamra Martinez, no frequency given. Safa'a LaRoche basically stated, '96 to 2000, every day; for a total of 1,825 times with Safa'a LaRoche. Krystal Harden alleged from '96 to 2000 3 to 4 times per week; total 1,040 times. The grand total of alleged sex acts from '93 to 2001 is 11,568 times; alleged sex acts per year 1,446 times; alleged sex acts per month 121 times. The age Malachi York would have been in 1993 is 48; the age he would have been in 2001 is 56. These numbers do not include the women that are in his main family. Now, I just pose a general, practical question to you: What is the likelihood that a gentleman who's 48, 56 years old -- no insult intended, but just a practical question -- would have sex 121 times per month continually for an eight-year period of time?

Another point I'd like to make with that frequency, additionally, practically speaking, how would Malachi York coordinate it so that David Noel would never see any girls and Amanda Noel would never see any boys and no-one would see Shilamooh? Remember, no-one saw Salaam LaRoche. No-one ever saw Shilamooh except Shilamooh. And it was a different witness that saw another person. Over an eight-year period of time or a ten-year period of time, with that frequency, it is no way one person could coordinate the schedule so that, that will happen. The only logical explanation is it didn't happen. Now, the government spoke to you somewhat about the instructions. I'll speak to you about that in a minute, but I want to briefly go over the government's witnesses that they've presented, and I'm going to start with Kenneth Lanning, the expert they presented. Now Kenneth Lanning basically stated that there were typologies of sexual offenders. He basically stated that a person that's a pedophile, or whatever, doesn't have to particularly have an age group they cater to; they don't particularly have to have a sex they cater to; that they could buy children or adults rings and things. Basically, what Kenneth Lanning is saying is that a person, as they're trying to describe Malachi York, would like young boys, young girls, adult women, adult men, all ages -- I don't think they allege adult men -- multiple sex partners, group orgies; and because he does anything, if he takes them out to eat, that means he's a sex offender. If he takes adult men out to eat, that means he's convincing the men to let him molest children. Basically, anything he did -- if he bought a girl a birthday gift, that was convincing her to have sex with him. If he bought a man a ring, that was convincing them. Basically, Kenneth Lanning described -- his description would basically fit anyone. So, our position would be that basically his findings were irrelevant and too broad, but I'll let you be the judge of that. Now, let's talk about

Nicole Lopez. Nicole Lopez clearly -- she had an immunity agreement, and the judge will instruct you on the immunity agreement. Just a second. The Court will instruct you that some witness' testimony must be considered with more caution than the testimony of other witnesses. The Judge will instruct you, for example, that [READING] a paid informer or a witness who has been promised that he or she would not be charged or prosecuted, or a witness who hopes to gain more favorable treatment in his or her own case, may have reason to make a false statement because the witness wants to strike a good bargain with the government. While such a witness of that kind may be entirely truthful when testifying, you should consider that testimony with more caution than the testimony of other witnesses. Now, the Judge will instruct you on that, and it's a very important point to remember, because the crux of the government's case relies upon two people that have immunity agreements, Nicole Lopez and Abigail Washington. Now, Mr. Moultrie stated that he was unfamiliar with the language about favorable concessions in the document. That's just another example of the carelessness of the government in this case. They're not even familiar with what they're offering the witnesses to testify. Clearly, Abigail Washington was told that she would receive favorable concession -- actually, I don't have it there (indicating) --in this case. She was looking for favorable concessions, and that's what she would receive, so take any statement by her, Nicole Lopez, in that regard.

Now, Nicole Lopez stated, yes, she went to Southbeach, Florida; also yes, she was in the bed with Lemuel LaRoche, Safa'a LaRoche's brother, but that's no big deal; they were just playing around. Also, she was with Noah Eddington, which is Shilamooh and Khalid Eddington's brother. That's no big deal; they were just playing around. She stated also that it was a big Joke to them, that they even laughed about it. They even e-mailed Malachi York pictures of the South Beach trip because it was funny. Also Nicole Lopez needed this immunity agreement because she was sleeping with two under age boys, Kuwsh Martinez and Esam. Now, let's go to Khalid Eddington. I've presented several boys that lived with Khalid Eddington. Khalid

Eddington gave you a story about how he bled and he went back to the restroom and stayed all night. I presented at least four witnesses that lived in the boy's house with Khalid Eddington that never saw this instance; also stated that if he would've come in after curfew, that would've been a very noticeable thing. No-one noticed this. No-one supports this allegation. Also, Salha Eddington, she testified. She testified that when she was taken from the land, she stated, "No, nothing happened to me." She stated continually on at least three different occasions. It wasn't until she got with her father that she changed her story. Her father is Bruce LaRoche, which is Khalid Eddington -- Salaam LaRoche's father, Noah Eddington's father. When asked, "Didn't you call one of your friends and say one of the reasons you changed your story was because your father pressured you," and she said yes. Now, David Noel testified that he did tell Manny Arora that he changed his story because his mother pressured him to. Then he said he felt some pressure from Wilford Buckley. Well, that's when we called his sister in to testify, his sister, who said, "Yes, David told me that he was pressured by his mother and that the allegations weren't true." And David Noel is Nicole Adah Lopez' brother and Amanda Noel's brother. Now, they put up Tomekia Pittman, and she basically stated that the purpose for money structuring would be to evade taxes, but we've clearly shown from the testimony, the accountant, that Malachi York has filed taxes for 30 years. Then Salaam LaRoche. No-one saw Salaam LaRoche at all. There's not one witness who said, "I saw something happen to Salaam LaRoche." He just has this one -- these few activities allegedly with Malachi York in the midst of these many times that everyone else is at Malachi York's home. Then Jin Hee Bae, Ginger Chang. First, she stated that it was Khalil, she stated, not Khalid until she read the FBI report. But the most interesting thing about Jin Bae's testimony is that she said she thinks she's dreaming or she doesn't know whether she's dreaming or reality, or something to that effect. So I just ask that you take that statement into consideration when weighing the validity of her testimony. Now, Ebony Hill, who's the person that corrected me when I asked her where she worked -- I asked her did she work at Javerty's (phonetic) she said, "No, I work at Goosebumps." Also, she stated she was involved in bank fraud but she didn't know it was illegal. Also, she left her son at the land that she's claiming is so dangerous. She left him there for six years and, to her knowledge, he's still there. And she stated that the land was safe for children.

Atiyah Thomas. Atiyah Thomas is seen here with Jacob York. She dated Jacob York. And this was in South Beach Miami. Now, Atiyah Thomas' mother and sister came to testify before you. Atiyah Thomas' mother stated that Atiyah Thomas has never told her she was molested by Malachi York. Atiyah Thomas' sister said she never saw any signs that Atiyah Thomas was molested and she never told her. And I ask that you weigh the value of the sister and the mother's testimony about their relative and the fact that she has a sexual relationship with Jacob York, as most of these alleged victims do. Now Sakinah Parham. Sakinah Parham has her own -- she had a sexual relationship with Jacob York. Also, she abused Harry (phonetic) Parham, which is Malachi York's son. She has her own case of child abuse. And she just recently recruited and influenced another witness, Arlene Hamilton and told her about the case and had her come testify. Now, Issa Johnson. Issa Johnson got on the stand and told you that none of these allegations ever happened, it just didn't happen. The government did put him up. And he's been saying that since the day the land was raided. He said, "I was not molested, nothing happened, I didn't see anything happen, it just didn't happen." Now, his caseworkers got on the stand, Janna Waddell, and said, "Oh, he told me he was touched or he was messed with for three years." Then I asked her, I said, "Do you have an audio tape or a videotape of that statement," because Issa Johnson told you, ladies and gentleman of the jury, that he was not molested, that nothing happened. Then Nicole Harden testified. She testified that she wrote her daughter a letter, talking about her daughter telling her she was pregnant from Esam, but that Malachi York caused her to write these letters to her daughter, and she also stated that she stole money from the office. Well, she said she took money from the office. I asked her, well, did she steal it. We got into it back and forth about stealing and taking. So, nevertheless, she stole money from the office. She's also one of the key witnesses, this person that stole money from the office, from the apartment complex, in the money-structuring charge. Then Qamra Muhammad. Qamra Muhammad is seen here with Jacob York at a nightclub in Atlanta. She couldn't remember exactly what nightclub it was. But she testified only to acts. I guess -- she already had a child and she was 16 at the time, she alleged, so technically, if you believe the sexual acts, there was no illegal sex at the time - And, also she's not one of the named alleged people -- alleged victims in the indictment. Now, Safa'a LaRoche. Safa'a LaRoche -- Safa'a LaRoche is under a heavy influence by Lemuel LaRoche, her brother, who's connected with Nicole Lopez. Now, her brother Ziyaad LaRoche and her mother stated, when they testified, that they'd never seen any signs that Safa'a LaRoche was molested. And a very key thing her mother said was that, once she asked Safa'a whether she was a virgin in 2000, and she said yes -- okay -- which a daughter may tell her mother that and that might not be true. But, more importantly, her mother said before she left Atlanta, she wanted to say goodbye to Malachi York, and she said it just didn't seem as if you'd want to say goodbye to someone that has been molesting you like that. But I'll let you weigh the value of that, a mother and a brother saying that they do not believe she was molested.

Now, Krystal Harden testified, and she basically stated to you that she lied to her mother about being pregnant by Esam just to make her mad. She also stated that her mother did beat her. So, I mean, you can -- I'll just let you be the judge and value her testimony. I mean, she basically said she -- she just lied and really didn't have a problem when she told her, in a very matter-of-fact tone, "Well, I lied to my mother because I wanted to make her mad." Also, Krystal Harden, through Amanda Noel's testimony, was also involved in stealing alcohol from one of the residences and stealing money from the finance office. And the government put up several witnesses to say that this could be symptoms of post-traumatic stress syndrome, but I asked the doctor, I said, "Also could this be -- could the trauma be physical abuse?" And they stated yes. And she admitted that her mother beats her. And, plus, we had an additional witness in our case to speak of the abuse by her mother to Krystal Harden. Also, Amanda Noel testified, and she stated basically a series of events that took place. The one very important thing about Amanda Noel, when she went for evaluation at the doctor, she stated that she had no previous sexual partners and the doctor said she takes very meticulous notes, and if she stated that she put it in her report, that's what Amanda told her. However, Amanda told you on the stand that she had two other consensual sexual partners and that she never told the doctor that. I will let you weigh the value of whether or not Amanda Noel is a truthful person. Now, Muniyra Franklin testified yesterday, and she testified to several allegations of molestation by Malachi York. But she did write two affidavits, and it states, "I was being very naive to the situation when I was coerced into this by Habiybah Washington. She said that I should talk to the FBI and tell them I had sexual intercourse with Malachi York, at the same time saying" -- this is after he was arrested -- nothing ever happened to me; he is like a father." October 23rd, 2003. There's an additional affidavit which she wrote, "I, Muniyra Franklin, have no idea why people, whoever they are, are making these false allegations against Malachi York and using my name. I'm letting it be known to whomever that I look at this man as a father figure. Never have I known this man to act inappropriately towards me. He has always been a role model and a father to me. Anything you've heard that I said is all false. I felt pressured and I was naive to the situation. So anything that involves me pertaining to this ridiculous case is all false...."

Now Arlene Hamilton testified to an incident where she said Malachi York -- well, that Ebony Henry had oral sex with Malachi York. However, Arlene Hamilton was contacted by Sakinah Parham, and Arlene Hamilton also had sexual relations with Jacob York... Basically, at some point, her and Sakinah Parham talked, and I guess Sakinah told her, "Hey, you need to come down and give the jury a few more people to testify against Malachi York," because she gave her number to the courthouse, and she called, and I guess they made arrangements.

Now, one very important thing Arlene Hamilton told you is that she lived with Jacob York and that there was a meeting or a few meetings with Jacob York, Atiyah Thomas, Sakinah Parham, her, and several other people in relation to this case. That's very important because she stated that she read the newspaper about the case and she was able to identify who was making a statement by the statement they made. The only way you can do that is to already know the statement that they were going to make, because there were no names. Now, you may be wondering why people or how could all of these allegations come up with so many people. Well, I would surmise from our investigation of the case is that there are a few conspirators that are connected in the case. You have Jacob York, his sister. Jacob York's sister, Leah Mabry, testified that Jacob York had at his house -- it was Barbara Noel, David Noel, Amanda Noel, Atiyah Thomas, Nicole Adah Lopez, and that basically Jacob York has a vendetta against his father, he hates him, and he's the only one of Malachi York's children that hates him. Also Abigail Washington, in her testimony, I asked her was there a class action suit where Jacob York was recruiting people to file against Malachi York, and she said yes. Also, he's had sexual relationships or close relationships with several of these alleged victims or witnesses -- Atiyah Thomas, Nicole Adah Lopez, Sakinah Parham, Arlene Hamilton, Qamra Muhammad, Abigail Washington. Also, it's very important to know that Jacob York and Barbara Noel had a home together, and they're very intricately involved in creating the allegations against Malachi York. Now, Abigail Washington, she was basically stripped of her financial power after several misdeeds with the money and kids, and so forth and so on. She indicated to you that she was negotiating a book deal and that it even got to the point of talking about money. Also, her immunity agreement, which you'll have as evidence, states that she's given her statement for favorable concessions. There's only one interpretation of "favorable concessions" to me. It must be for money. Also, she was ousted by the community. You've got Nicole

Adah Lopez... she had a sexual relationship with Jacob York, she molested several underage boys -- Kuwsh Martinez, which Qamra Muhammad's brother, and Esam -- all unknown to Malachi York. She hosted parties with underage children, including Amanda Noel and Krystal Harden. The party that I'm talking about was the party that was in the sewing room when her mother was in the other room, and they were drinking alcohol and having sex, all while Malachi York was not present. He was in Athens. Nicole Lopez was ousted from the community.

Then you have Amanda Noel. She was strongly influenced by her sister Nicole Adah Lopez, pressured by her mother Barbara Noel, as David Noel was, and she's close friends with Krystal Harden, Rodeya Herbert, Safa'a LaRoche, and Muniyra Franklin. And, also, she stole from the main house and money from the finance department. She lied about the number of sexual partners to the medical doctor, claimed she had no other sexual partners. Sakinah Parham; she had a sexual affair with Jacob York. She filed a lawsuit against Malachi York. She physically abused and was arrested for child abuse of Harry Parham, Malachi York's child, and just last week influenced and recruited Arlene Hamilton to testify at the last minute. Now, Nicole Harden; she admitted that she stole money from the community property. She was stripped of power. She's a friend with Abigail Washington. She physically abused her daughter Krystal Harden. She stated her daughter Krystal Harden is a frequent liar. And she was ousted from the Community. Now, Atiyah Thomas; she had a sexual relationship with Jacob York. She's friends with Nicole Adah Lopez and Abigail Washington and Lemuel LaRoche -- I'm sorry -- and Abigail Washington. Now, Lemuel LaRoche, he had a sexual relationship with Nicole Adah Lopez, a very strong influence on Safa'a LaRoche. Okay. Now, I want to show you the entire chart, and this will be everyone that the government has presented to you as witnesses in the case: Jacob York, Sakinah Parham, Arlene Hamilton, Atiyah Thomas, Suhaila Williams, Barbara Noel, Qamra Muhammad, Nicole Adah Lopez -- her mother is Barbara Noel; brother is David Noel -- Amanda Noel, friend... I should have brought it over --- Krystal Harden, Rodeya Herbert, Safa'a LaRoche, Lemuel LaRoche and Noah Eddington are in pictures of Nicole Lopez in South Beach. And Lemuel LaRoche and Noah Eddington, they all brought in the LaRoche family, which is Salha Eddington, Kiturah Eddington; Khalid Eddington, Salaam LaRoche, Safa'a LaRoche. And Abigail Washington worked in the finance office with Nicole Harden. And Muniyra Franklin indicated in an affidavit that Abigail Washington was the one that forced her to make false allegations against Malachi York. Then Jin Hee Bae, she just basically stated she had a dream. She's not sure that whatever happened is a dream or reality. Now, I went over a lot of information with you, and I understand that was quite extensive. However, it's that type of case where there's a lot of information to be gone over. Now, I'm going to briefly discuss one or two other things and I'll close. I want to talk to you about overt acts. Now, count one of the indictment, was talking about a general -- it's a general conspiracy count. The one thing in your decision about this case is that you have to be convinced that the intent of any travel on any highway, if this organization was going to relocate from New York to Georgia, you have to believe that all these people that got on this stand came down to Georgia for the purpose of molesting children, that Malachi York said, "Hey, let's all go down to Georgia because we're going to molest children." Basically, you have to find that. That is the crime. Actually, as Richard Moultrie stated to you, child molestation is not the crime here. It's whether or not there was an intent, while traveling, to molest children. So, basically, the government would have to show that any travel from New York to Georgia, from Georgia to Disney World, was for that purpose. I want to refer you to one thing for your consideration. In an arraignment and detention hearing on May 9th, 2002 A.D. under sworn testimony --

Mr. Moultrie - "Your Honor, he can't read something that's not in evidence as part of his closing statement."
Mr. Patrick - "Your Honor, I crossed Jalaine Ward on this transcript."
Mr. Moultrie - "But that wasn't tendered as a document."

BIOGRAPHICAL REBUTTAL TO PEOPLE MAGAZINE

Mr. Patrick - *"Your Honor, I mean, I asked her these questions. I can read this. And this is my closing argument, and you're going to instruct the jury"*

Mr. Moultrie - *"Your Honor, it's not a document that is in evidence. It's a hearsay document."*

Mr. Patrick - *"Your Honor, I cross examined her on this document while she was on the stand, and it came out in the case."*

The Court - *"I think that you are restricted to -- well, wait a minute"*

Mr. Patrick - *"Well, can I just summarize what I --"*

The Court - *"Yeah, you can summarize. There's no problem with that.*

Mr. Patrick - *"All right. Basically, in the arraignment and detention hearing May 9, 2002 A.D. Jalaine Ward stated -- upon being asked "Whether or not you have any witnesses to testify to the fact that the purpose of the interstate travel was for sex with children, "Jalaine Ward stated "no." Now, I want to point out another important thing to you because, actually, the charges to me are very confusing and they're very complex charges....All right. A very important part of the charge is where it outlines an overt act. Mr. Moultrie told you that they quoted over 80 overt acts in the indictment. That's true, But there is a key concept here; that an overt act is any transaction event, even one, which may be entirely innocent when considered alone. In other words, an overt act can just be anything that's legal or whatever. However, Richard Moultrie left you with the -- the government -- I'll not call his name individually. The government left you with the impression that all you have to do is find the commission of an overt act; whether legal or illegal, it doesn't matter. That's not true. There is another key component of that. You have to think that that overt act was knowingly committed by a conspirator in an effort to accomplish some objective of the conspiracy, a key concept. If you believe, for example, that Malachi York impregnated Habibah Washington and he did that alone which is not illegal, that would also mean that you would have to believe that because he impregnated Habibah Washington and they had kids later, or whatever, that that means that he was molesting children throughout the organization.*

But the pure act itself is not illegal. But what the government wants to leave you the impression is that "if we prove just one of the 80 acts, he's guilty of conspiracy." That's not true. The very first question you have to decide is whether or not you believe that all 42 witnesses that got on that stand in the defense's case and testified on behalf of the defendant were in this organization and that the defendant some way convinced them to travel interstate commerce for him to molest children, when each one of the witnesses told you that it was a voluntary decision and not everyone came down to Eatonton. You have members in London -- this is very important -- have members in London, Chicago, and everything. There was no requirement whatsoever that you had to go to Eatonton. So the first thing you must decide is whether or not you believe that the purpose of the interstate travel, whether it was from New York to Georgia to Disney, was for that purpose to molest children. And the government said that doesn't have to be the only purpose, but they're saying that's a substantial purpose. You have to believe that Evelyn Rivera, Samiyra Samad, all of those individuals, were in this organization assisting Malachi York in molesting children. So it's another key element which is you have to believe -- that the overt act, not the overt act, itself -- if you believe that act, you have to also believe -- you have to first believe that there was a conspiracy to molest children in interstate commerce. So it's very important. And it's very easy to get confused about; to me, it was; but I hope I've explained that to you and you'll take note of that during your deliberations, because the government has not presented any witnesses that can tell you that the purpose of the interstate travel was for the purpose of molesting children. They cannot prove that to you, and they have not shown that to you. Now, just a few other points I'd like to make. There was some mention of food, education problems. I presented several witnesses to you -- we presented 42 witnesses. I think the government presented 43 witnesses - I think I presented 42 witnesses in four days. But what I was trying to show you is the diverse membership in this organization. You have international members; you have older members, younger members; you have kids; and everybody states that they ate and that they were educated. One thing you would have to note about all of the witnesses that are a part of this organization, everybody was well-spoken and well-behaved. Those are the type of principles that were taught in this organization. Now, whether or not you necessarily agree with certain beliefs they may have, that's irrelevant to the issue of interstate travel for the purpose of criminal activity. Because, in the United States of America, the beautiful thing about us is anybody can believe anything they want to believe, and the government is supposed to protect that right, not attack that right. Now what I want to do -- and I'll close out -- is point out another very basic thing to you. The government didn't present you any photos of children being molested, but there are tons of photos of children being happy in this case. This has to be the happiest set of child molested victims in the world. And I want to show you, from the government's side, the pictures they presented you. These are not my pictures; these are the government's pictures.

(PAUSE FOR VIDEOGRAPHER)

Mr. Patrick - *That's Amanda Noel, happy. That's Sakinah Woods and Safa'a LaRoche. That's David Noel. That's Safa'a LaRoche. This is just a group of kids on the land happy. This is Safa'a LaRoche, Suhaila Thomas. They're in the pool having fun. This is Abigail Washington smiling, Safa'a LaRoche smiling, and Husna Evans. But this is the main bedroom when Malachi York was NOT living there. But, nevertheless, I'm trying to go to the point that they're happy. Those are the government's photos. That's Atiyah Thomas and Sakinah Parham. That's Atiyah Thomas again -- can we get it clear? Maybe it's just out of focus*

(PAUSE FOR VIDEOGRAPHER)

Mr. Patrick - *"But, anyway, that's Atiyah Thomas. It's blurry. All right. That's Atiyah Thomas, Suhaila Thomas, and Ms. Thomas. Atiyah Thomas, Suhaila Thomas, Setheenese Thomas, Salha*

Eddington, Abigail Washington. Abigail Washington, Ebony Henry; and I'm not sure. This is the Drayton Family that both testified, Mr. and Mrs. Drayton, and their son. That's Khalid Eddington. That's Ziyaad LaRoche, And that's Zidou (phonetic), I believe. That's Safa'a LaRoche in one of the homes. That's Safa'a LaRoche and Hajar Cosme, Mildred Cosme's daughter. That's Krystal Harden. That's Issa Johnson. There's several other individuals in the picture, a group of kids. There's another group of kids. That's Salha Eddington, Hajar Cosme. Suhaila Thomas, Krystal Harden. This is Jacob York. And I'd like to show you one other exhibit if you could.

(Playing Videotape for Jury)

Mr. Patrick - *"Ladies and gentleman, I urge you find the only fair verdict in this case, and that's a verdict of not guilty, Thank you."*

Conclusion

"My mission and it's gonna be difficult and I'm going to be hated, but I'm in good company when I'm hated because they hated all of the men The Most High sent. If they like me, I know I'm doing something wrong, you understand? I'm going to be hated. I'm going to be slandered. I'm going to be reviled. People are gonna say all manners of evil against me falsely. I expect all that. I accept all that.... Jesus was persecuted because he did not follow the law of his day. So why are Christians not being persecuted? But we Nuwaupians are being persecuted because we're trying to follow the law of the Bible. Blessed is he who is persecuted for righteous namesake, for great is his reward in heaven for so persecuted they the prophets which were before you. That's the deal. The deal is if you decide to pick up your cross and follow the law, the law of Moses and the grace and truth of Jesus Christ. You are going to be persecuted. They are going to persecute you. They're going to revile thee and say all manners of evil against you falsely. They're gonna slander you. They're gonna drag you to court. They're gonna call you a cult. They're gonna have many people [saying] "yeah, yeah, yeah" because Satan got a host of people that cheer him on. A bunch of black devils, a bunch of white devils, young & old who infiltrate your organization, live with you, love with you, eat with you, dine with you, party with you and they're the children of the devil. They can come through your own seed. The devil gets inside people and takes control. That's why Jesus said he had to cast out legions of devils from people. The Romans persecuted Jesus not just the Devil. The devil came out but so were the Romans

all tempting him, chasing him, trying to kill him. His own black folks, the so-called Nazarites stoned him. You're gonna get all of that. But if you have a Church out there and a Preacher that everybody loves and everybody's cheering him on and he's got his own television program and everything's looking all so sweet, no persecution, no Sheriffs coming after him, no slander; That man is not doing the right thing because they tell you right in the Bible you're gonna be persecuted after righteousness sake. Matthew 5:10-12 "Blessed are they which are persecuted for righteousness' sake: for theirs is the kingdom of heaven. Blessed are ye, when men shall revile you, and persecute you, and shall say all manner of evil against you falsely, for my sake. Rejoice, and be exceedingly glad; for great is your reward in heaven; for so persecuted they the prophets which were before you." You hear that? That's the plight of a Nuwaupian. Nuwaupian is not a person, Nuwaupian is a race. People of all colors belong to Nuwaupians."
~ **Dr. Malachi Z. York**

Dr. York has a right to be who and what he is and you have a right to not accept him BUT you do **NOT** have a right to falsely accuse, slander, torture, wrongfully convict, wrongfully imprison and character assassinate **AN INNOCENT MAN**.

Revelation Chapter 17:14
"<u>These shall make war with the Lamb,</u> **and the Lamb shall overcome them**<u>; for he is Lord of lords, and King of Kings; and they that are with him are called, and chosen, and faithful."</u>
Amen.

About the Author

DonVito Harold Long is a Nuwaupian Yamassee Native American who lives on The Land.

Bibliography

King James Holy Bible. 1611 A.D.

Dr. York. Persecution Of The Leaders, Sermon

Minister Louis Farrakhan Reveals To The World "The Reformer" York, As Sayyid Issa Al Haadi Al Mahdi. YouTube

Dr. York. The Savior Edition 1

Dr. York. The Book of the FIVE PERCENTERS, 1991 A.D

Dr. York. Evil Invaders From Egipt To America, Go Home!, Sermon

The Ancient Ones. Egypt Of The West Newsletter Edition 1 Volume 22, August 30, 1998 A.D.

Dr. York. THE AKASHA RECORDS, Series No.72

I.D. Channel. People Magazine Investigates Cults: The United Nuwaubian Nation of Moors, July 9, 2018 A.D.

Dr. York. The Ansaar Cult Rebuttal to the Slanderers, 1989 A.D.

Dr. York. Message to the Black Man, True Light Sermon

Dr. York. The Holy Tablets, 1996 A.D.

Letteschat. I Survived Living in a Cult - A true Story by Ruby Garnett. Blog Talk Radio, 6-20-2013 A.D.

Ruby Garnett. Soul Sacrifice: One Story of Many, 2011 A.D.

Bilal Phillips. The Ansar Cult in America, 1988 A.D.

Dr. York. The Sacred Wisdom of Tehuti, Circa 2000 A.D.

Dr. York. Ahmad Jesus' Khalifat (Successor), 1980 A.D.

Dr. York. The Holy Tabernacle Family Guide, 1994 A.D.

Dr. York. Help Jesus Separate The Sheep From The Goat, Sermon

Dennis Hevesi. Muslims Leave Bushwick; The Neighbors Ask Why, The New York Times, April 24, 1994 A.D.

USA vs YORK Trial Testimony: Case 5:02-CR-27-CAR), 2004 A.D.

Farah Muhammad. Eyewitness Conspiracy Video, June 1, 2004 A.D.

Habiba "Abigail" Washington. Video Recant Of False Trial Testimony, April 18, 2004 A.D.

Maulana Muhammad Ali. Holy Quran Seventh Edition, 1991 A.D.

Case 5:02-cr-00027-CAR Document 407-17 Filed 3/02/09

Dr. York. The Millennium Book Part 2, 2000 A.D.

New York Times. "Jean Vanier, Savior of The People on The Margins, Dies at 90."

Jimmy Breslin. "Combatting Crime By Force-of Will," Newsday, June 1, 1989 A.D.

Dr. York. Does Dr. Malachi Z. York try to hide the fact that he was Imaam Issa?, 1996 A.D.

Dr. York. The Man of Miracles In This Day And Time, 1983 A.D.

Dr. York. Who and What are You? True Light Sermon

Case 5:02-CR-00027-CAR Document 417 Filed 4/02/09

Sylvester Monroe. Space Invaders - Time Magazine, July 12, 1999 A.D.

Hilary Hiliard & Rob Peecher. Accusation of Racism - The Macon Telegraph, August 8, 1999 A.D.

Joe Johnson. Man Pleads not guilty in 16-year old alleged Athens murder - ATHENS BANNER - HERALD, September 20, 2018 A.D.

Dr. York. Part 6 of Dr Malachi Z. York in 1992 - Sermon

Dr. York. Is The Root Of The Devil In Our Children?, Sermon

Dr. York. Do Women Have Souls According To The Bible, Sermon

The United States of America VS. Dwight D. York and Kathy Johnson, DEFENDANTS 5:02-CR-27(HL) May 9, 2002 A.D & May 13-14 2002 A.D. Arraignment & Detention Hearing

Dr. York. The New Covenant, Sermon

Dr. York. Why We Used Islam, Sermon

Dr. York. The Sons of Canaan, 1987 A.D.

Case 5:02-CR-00027-CAR Document 382 Filed 6-27-07

liberiafreedryork.com

Dr. York. It's On Me - British Television Performance

Tama-Re - Egypt Of The West, Eatonton, Georgia

De La Soul. Stakes Is High Album Cover & Liner Notes, 1996 A.D.

The Chosen Ones. Enter The Lord Album Cover, 1989 A.D.

Redhead Kingpin and THE F.B.I. Do The Right Thing Album Cover, 1989 A.D.

Ansaar Nubian Flag Medallion

Public Enemy. Fear of a Black Planet Album Cover & Liner Notes, 1990 A.D.

Doug E. Fresh. "A Proud Nubian" sweatshirt

Grandmaster Melle Mel & Van Silk. What's the matter with your World, Video

KMD. Peach Fuzz, Video

The Source - Magazine of hip-hop music, culture & Politics. August 1997 A.D.

Bobby Bennett and Jimmy Smith. Billboard Magazine, May 1985 A.D.

New Directions for York's Productions INC. Promo Display Ad, 1988 A.D.

The Scientists of Sound. Picture of 6 pointed Star and Crescent of Ansaarullah Community

The Lost Children of Babylon. Martial Law Video Photo & Photo in front of Black Pyramid on Tama-Re - Egypt of the West, Eatonton, Georgia.

Jaz-O. Originators Video

Twista. Runnin off at da Mouth Album Cover, 1992 A.D. & Song - "Say What"

Killah Priest. The Psychic World of Walter Reed Album Cover, 2013 A.D.

Drawing of Dr. York with the Seal of Yaanuwn glowing in left hand and Sham on his right above his head.

Killah Priest. Behind the Stained Glass, song

Prodigy & Lost Children of Babylon member. Photo

Was Prodigy killed because of the facts he revealed about Dr. Malachi Z. York. Interview

Dr. York & James Ingram. Photo on Tama-Re - Egypt of The West, Eatonton, Georgia

Afrika Bambaataa. Return To Planet Rock Album Cover featuring Jungle Brothers.

Afrika Bambaataa & Zulu Nation members. Photo on Tama-Re - Egypt of The West, Eatonton, Georgia.

FinalCall.com. Rap COINTELPRO: Subverting the Power of Hip-Hop, July 3, 2011 A.D.

Mysteries Behind Closed Doors: The Untold Truth of the Dr. Malachi Z. York Case. 2010 A.D.

US Probation Office Report. NO. 7773

Hearing Before United States District Judge Hugh Lawson. June 30, 2003 A.D.

Dr. York. Maku Speaks from the Isles of Patmos. Telephone Interviews from Jail, 2004 A.D.

Dr. York. Din Allah or Dinul Islaam, Sermon

Dr. York. God's Law vs Man's Law, Sermon

PRESIDENT AND HEAD OF STATE OF THE
UNITED NUWAUPIAN NATION
CHIEF: BLACK "THUNDERBIRD" EAGLE

Our Constitutionally Seated President and Head of
The State of Nuwaupia, The United Nuwaupian
Nation of The Yamassee Native Americans, Creek,
Seminole, Shushuni, Washitaw
No. 215 - 1993   No. 208 - 1999
SOVEREIGN GRAND COMMANDER

H.E. Dr. Malachi Z. K. York - El 33/720

Declaration of Independence to the World on
June 26th 1992 A.D.

www.ingramcontent.com/pod-product-compliance
Lightning Source LLC
Chambersburg PA
CBHW022043160426
43209CB00002B/50